The Self-Esteem COMPANION

Simple Exercises to Help You Challenge Your Inner Critic & Celebrate Your Personal Strengths

MATTHEW MCKAY, PH.D.
PATRICK FANNING
CAROLE HONEYCHURCH
CATHARINE SUTKER

New Harbinger Publications, Inc.

Publisher's Note

This publication is designed to provide accurate and authoritative information in regard to the subject matter covered. It is sold with the understanding that the publisher is not engaged in rendering psychological, financial, legal, or other professional services. If expert assistance or counseling is needed, the services of a competent professional should be sought.

Distributed in Canada by Raincoast Books

Cover and text design by Amy Shoup

Library of Congress Cataloging-in-Publication Data

The self-esteem companion : simple exercises to help you challenge your inner critic and celebrate your personal strengths / Matthew McKay ... [et al.].
    p. cm.
 Originally published: 1999.
 ISBN-10 1-57224-411-9
 ISBN-13 978-1-57224-411-5
 1. Self-esteem. 2. Self-esteem—Problems, exercises, etc. I. McKay, Matthew.
 BF697.5.S46S45 2005
 158.1—dc22

                 2005018921

10   09   08

10   9   8   7   6   5

For Dana Landis
—M.M.

For the Monday night men's group
—P.F.

For Piki and Prudence
—C.H.

For my family
—C.S.

Contents

Preface

In my practice, I have found that wounded self-esteem is the root of most emotional problems. And the opposite is also true. Success stories begin with a sense of confidence, a belief in oneself. Self-esteem is the ingredient that makes strong and lasting relationships, builds a nurturing community, and turns dreams into achievements. It is the source of the sustained motivation we need to overcome obstacles, setbacks, and doubt.

Many people believe that their level of self-esteem is fixed and constant, that there's nothing they can do about feelings of low worth. This is untrue. How much or little you value yourself can change tremendously over time. You have the power to raise your sense of worth—not just a little, but a lot. The secret of building good self-esteem is to learn to see the whole you, not just your warts, failures and mistakes. What if you stopped focusing on what's wrong with you, and started paying attention to your strengths and assets, the moments in your life that you are proud of? Growing your self-esteem is about paying attention—to how you love, to what you give, to all the hard work of being alive.

This book will show you how to stop listening to that nattering voice inside that's always criticizing and putting you down. It will teach you how to silence those shaming thoughts that keep pounding you for every mistake. But most important, it will help you create a new, accepting voice that—like a good parent—validates you and gives you confidence. Every exercise in this book is a proven strategy that will build your worth and change how you see yourself.

But remember this: changing is not the same as wishing. If you want to raise your self-esteem, reading the book won't be enough. You'll have to actually do some of the exercises. You'll need to practice with these tools and techniques. I promise you—if you invest a little effort, your feelings about yourself will change. Your confidence will grow. Your life and your relationships will be profoundly different. All you have to do is turn the page and begin.

—Matthew McKay, Ph.D.

Introduction

What Is Self-Esteem, Anyway?

· ·

Have you ever seen a T-shirt that reads, "Life's a Beach?" It's a good image to help you understand self-esteem.

If you have high self-esteem, you place yourself higher up on the beach of life, safe from the waves, where there's plenty of room to spread out your stuff on dry sand. You're conveniently close to the snack bar, bathrooms, and volleyball net. You feel warm and relaxed. You can wander around, talk to people, eat an ice cream cone, flirt a little, go down to the water for a swim, have a good time.

If you have low self-esteem, you find yourself lower down on the beach of life, too close to the water, where it's damp, cold, and windy. You don't spread your stuff out very far because the bigger waves can reach you and engulf everything. You can see others having a good time, but you feel isolated, resentful of the people with better spots, and incapable of moving.

You might try to improve your situation by building walls of sand around you, but these defenses only isolate you further, and you know that the waves will eventually wash the walls away, no matter how high or how perfectly you build them. You might have a few beers, brag about your bravery, joke about your plight, get mad, or make excuses. But nothing helps to stem your growing awareness that the tide is rising.

If you don't like your spot on the self-esteem beach, you can start to improve your situation right now by taking this short quiz. It will help you begin to see how self-esteem operates in your life. Check the statements that are mostly true for you:

1. I would rather stay home than go to a party.

2. I sometimes overindulge in alcohol, drugs, tobacco, or food.

3. I dress conservatively so I won't stand out.

4. I feel it's important to justify my actions to others.

5. I think a lot about how others are perceiving me.

6. I like a good argument for its own sake.

7. I don't push myself forward or take risks at work or school.

8. I often feel angry at other people.

9. I find it hard to say no to people.

10. I enjoy telling others about my successes.

The statements with odd numbers are meant to start you thinking about the ways low self-esteem makes you avoid certain people, situations, or feelings. Those with even numbers suggest ways you might feel compelled to defend against low self-esteem. These patterns can change. The rest of this book is about strengthening your sense of self-worth so these old defenses are no longer necessary.

PART I

Feel Better Fast

I n this section there are nine simple and easy exercises that will help you feel better about yourself fast. Thousands of people have used these techniques over the years and consistently proven their effectiveness in boosting self-esteem. These core secrets include remembering better times, giving yourself credit for your contributions to others, using mnemonic devices for recalling positive memories, staying relaxed from moment to moment, creating your own images for stress reduction, discovering hidden treasures in your life, consulting your inner guide, visualizing your true self-worth, and mastering a simple form of hypnotic suggestion.

Five-Finger Exercise

· · · · · · · · · · · · ·

Some days, especially when you're feeling particularly gloomy and down on yourself, you just need a quick, simple pick-me-up. You can use the five-finger exercise anytime to remember how to feel great about yourself.

Take three or four deep breaths; let feelings of relaxation and calm spread throughout your entire body. Let all of your muscles release their tension as you close your eyes. Now, as you continue to relax, become aware of your dominant hand.

This is called the five-finger exercise, but it's really about your four fingers and your thumb. Touch your thumb to your index finger. As you do, think back to your past, to a time when you felt really cared for and loved. Maybe it was when you had that stomachache and your parent took such good care of you. How about the time your friends threw you a big birthday party? Any time will do, whether it's a big event or a small moment.

Next, touch your thumb to your middle finger. Think back to a time you felt really successful. Was it your graduation from school? How about when you got your job or promotion? Or, maybe it was when your kids were born. Again, any time will do, as long as it provides a strong memory of your feelings of success.

Touch your thumb to your ring finger and remember a time that you did something important for someone else. Maybe it's taking care of a sick neighbor or baby-sitting for your sister's kids. It can be any moment of selflessness that's important to you.

Finally, touch your thumb to your pinkie and look for a memory of loving someone else. Think back to a moment when you felt love for another very strongly, when that feeling filled your heart.

Practice this exercise, and use it whenever you need a quick reminder of how to feel good.

It's a Wonderful Life

• • • • • • • • • • • • • •

Remember a desperate Jimmy Stewart on the bridge? And how an angel showed him an alternate reality—his town, his friends, his family as they would be if he had never lived. He learned that the world would be a darker place without him.

Sometimes it's easy to forget all the positive ways you touch the lives of others. You may not be a famous author or the CEO of a company, but your life matters. Your family, your friends, and even your acquaintances and work colleagues are affected by you in big and little ways.

A key element of self-esteem is to know you have a place in the world and no one else could fill it in quite the same way as you. Right now, make a list of all the people in your life—past and present—whom you have somehow touched. This can range from close family to someone you helped with math in the third grade; from your truest friend to the security guard you greet at work. Write down every name you can think of.

Next to each name, list one or more ways you have given that person something positive. It doesn't matter whether it's big or small, yesterday or forty years ago. It doesn't even matter whether they'd acknowledge or remember it. What matters is that *you* remember it.

Somewhere amid the routines, the struggles, the failures, and the moments of great pain, you can find that yours is a wonderful life. Sometimes it's difficult to see this, but it's true. This reality can be found. It can finally be celebrated.

Anchoring to the Good Times

· · · · · · · · · · · · · · · · · ·

Facing pain is a skill. If you know how pain works and how to cope with it, your actual encounters with pain will be less overwhelming. When you feel pain, all you can think about is *now*, and it's hard to imagine being okay again. At these times, all you want to do is escape. When you find yourself feeling this way, there's a technique you can use to combat the bad feelings—it's called *anchoring*.

Anchoring helps you reexperience times when you felt confident and good about yourself. An anchor is a stimulus that evokes feelings from specific events in the past. For instance, if you think of your grandmother's love and protection whenever you eat freshly made oatmeal cookies, then oatmeal cookies are an anchor for you. The cookies are the stimulus, and the feelings of love and safety are your consistent response. Of course, many of your anchors are involuntary, but you can form voluntary ones to use to your advantage. All you have to do is touch yourself on the wrist to remember the positive anchor you've formed.

Alex, a thirty-year-old artist, uses this technique. Even as a young child, he expressed his artistic nature in almost everything he did. His family first noticed his artistic inclinations when, at age two, he created an elaborate mural that covered most of his parent's expensive, tan leather couch. His parents replaced the couch with a less expensive version, but they saved the leather couch, keeping it in his room as a reminder of his earliest work.

As an adult, Alex went into the art world, where not everyone was so supportive and encouraging of his art. It was hard to establish himself as a professional artist—critics sometimes gave unkind reviews of his work, some gallery openings turned out to be a bust, and so on. However, Alex established an anchor for himself that he could use whenever he felt discouraged or his internal critic went on the attack.

He retired comfortably somewhere and did an exercise in which he would touch his wrist and visualize the couch that his parents always kept in his room as a reminder to him of his intrinsic artistic nature. He remembered the colors on the couch—the green swirls, orange thrashing lines, and yellow dots. Alex would breathe deeply, and as he was able to once again feel his confidence in himself, his true passion for art would flood his body and allow him to keep going and face the struggles that came his way.

Take a moment right now to try this easy but powerful exercise:

1. Sit in a comfortable position in a place where you won't be disturbed. Close your eyes and relax your body, breathing deeply into any areas you notice are tight.

2. Go back in time. Picture a moment when you felt successful or especially confident. Notice everything about that time: the sights, sounds, tastes, smells, and feelings. See how you looked, how others looked. Hear the confidence in your voice; hear the praise from others. Let yourself *feel* the confidence and self-acceptance.

3. When your images are clear enough to make you feel confident, touch your left wrist with your right hand. Touch it firmly, in a particular spot that you can easily remember. You are anchoring your feelings to this touch on your wrist, and you want to exactly duplicate that touch later on.

Repeat this sequence with four other memories or fantasy scenes that are connected to feelings of worth and self-confidence. After you have anchored to your own personal good times, you can touch your wrist whenever you need to fight a negative feeling. Your positive memories or fantasies are resources that you can call up anytime you need them. Now you can combat negative feelings and images with a touch that anchors you to some very fine moments in your life.

Honoring Your Body

. . . .

Have you ever just been walking along when you suddenly notice that you've been holding your shoulders tight and high for who knows how long? Or that you haven't taken a deep breath in hours? Or that you never relaxed your clenched jaw muscles after someone flipped you off in the car earlier in the day? Your body is always talking to you. It has a loud voice. It says things like "I'm tense," "I can't breathe," "I have a stomachache from that high-strung meeting today," or "I don't have enough energy to deal with my lousy job." Although you may try to, you can't ignore these messages for long. You can't help feeling the tension mount.

How relaxed are you right now? Can you feel tension in certain areas of your body? Sadly, if you're like most people, you're probably more aware of how much money you have in the bank or that your car is overdue for an oil change than you are of your own body. Well, it's time for that to change, time for you to listen to your body.

Your body can tell you about relaxation more than anyone else can. It knows your unique states of tension and release. Have you ever held a seashell up to your ear to hear the sea? In this same concentrated way, try listening carefully to yourself. Close your eyes and try to hear your body tell you what it's feeling. All you have to do is turn your attention within and quietly listen.

Go to a quiet spot and close your eyes. Allow your breathing to slow and deepen. Ask your body, "Where are you tense?" Scan your body for any tight neck or back muscles, sore joints, tiny aches and pains in your arms or legs, little twitches around your eyes, or places where you are hunched up to protect tender spots.

As you find each twitch or tension area, thank your body for showing it to you. Remember that all tension is muscular tension and all muscle contraction is self-produced, even when you aren't aware of producing it. So, once you become aware of the tension, you can begin to let it go. Focus on each area for a moment, exploring the tightness or soreness—even exaggerating it a little if you can. Exhale slowly and allow your tight back muscles to relax, your eyelids to stop twitching, your knees to stop aching. Tell your body, "It's okay, we can be peaceful for a moment. We can let go."

Once you've achieved a sense of relaxation in your body, remember to thank your body for keeping you alive and informed, for serving you despite all the times you've ignored its needs. Do something special for your body today. You'd do it for your car or your home, so why not for your physical self? Take a bubble bath, use your favorite body lotion, or wear your most comfortable cotton clothes. Or maybe you can go to the market and get something to make a really wholesome meal. Keep checking in with your body regularly. It will tell you what you need to feel nourished and cleansed.

Freeing Your Body

· · · · · · · · · · · · · ·

People experience emotions in their bodies as well as their minds. Do you ever get "gut feelings" about things? Have you ever been very angry and felt your stomach clenching? Or experienced sadness as a heaviness in your chest?

Even chronic feelings of low self-esteem can manifest in your body. You may feel the hollowness of failure in your stomach, the pressure of self-blame on your heart, or the pain of shame in your throat. You may have a painful hunch to your shoulders from a fear of rejection.

The following exercise can help free your body of feelings connected to low self-esteem. You may want to tape-record the exercises for repeated use.

The first step is to relax your body and mind. Sit or lie down in a quiet place, close your eyes, and begin to breathe slowly and deeply. Mentally check in with your body, scanning your muscles for signs of tension. If you find any tense areas, take a breath and release the tightness as you exhale. Remember to scan your whole body—your face, chest, back, arms, stomach, pelvis, and legs.

When you feel physically relaxed, try to quiet your mind. Clear out the random thoughts that dart in and out, and concentrate on a sense of stillness. If thoughts intrude, simply let them come and watch them go, always returning your focus to the quietness of your mind. Now you're ready to begin the visualization to clear your body of emotion-based pain.

Visualize the negative feelings that lie in your body. Give them a shape and a color. Make them as ugly and weird as you want. They could look like an anvil, a sword, a sack of potatoes, or an empty cave. Take some deep breaths. With each breath, see those feelings move out of your body and away from you. Watch the anvil leave your stomach or the choking fingers let go of your throat. You are floating past the bad feelings now. They are out of your body, and you are drifting away from them. They get farther and farther away from you. Keep focusing on your breathing as the negative feelings move farther away, first becoming a distant speck, then finally disappearing altogether.

Say to yourself: "These are feelings from the past. They come up whenever a situation arises that challenges me. I will survive them, floating past until my body is free from all of the pain."

In your imagination, step outside of yourself. Now you can see how bad you've felt. You can see how you struggle with those negative feelings in your torso and limbs. See your face, the position of your body. Imagine the location of any remaining negative feelings as a red glow in your body. It will fade in a while. Take deep breaths as you watch the red glow diminish. Imagine the bad feelings passing as the glow gradually fades away. If you wish, you can turn the red light into a neutral or relaxing color—pale blue or another gentle pastel. When you are ready, go back inside yourself.

Finally, envision a mental picture of yourself days or even years from now when these bad feelings are long gone. See yourself standing straight and tall, head up, confident, and relaxed. As you bring your awareness back to a more relaxed present moment, remember that you can do this exercise whenever your body is experiencing tension or pain from emotional stress.

Treasure Chest Visualization

· · · · · · · · · · · · · · · · · ·

Sometimes, when you're down on yourself, the feelings seem to come from a place so deep inside that you wonder if you'll ever be able to reach it and heal. In fact, you *can* reach that deep place and find the keys to unlock a treasure chest of positive feelings about yourself.

The following visualization will help you plumb deep into your unconscious to find some of your most precious, yet hidden, qualities.

Begin by sitting or lying down and closing your eyes for about five minutes. Try to empty your mind of everyday thoughts, welcoming an inner quiet. When a distracting thought arises, simply acknowledge it and wait for it to pass, and then return to your quiet mind.

Shift your attention to your body, scanning your muscles for sites of tension. When you encounter a tight area, take a deep breath. Then, on the exhale, release the tension. You will notice as you let go that your body is becoming warm and heavy. Now you're ready to travel to your treasure chest.

Imagine that you are strolling through a wide field of golden grass. The day is warm, and the sun caresses your shoulders. Listen to the sound of the warm breeze rustling the field of gold. A bird rises from the grass and flies overhead, calling out in a musical tone.

You start to follow a narrow path that leads to the edge of a lush forest. The rich soil is soft under your feet. The forest is cool and deep green. Sun filters in through the treetops, sometimes bursting through in golden beams to warm your face.

You step over a clear, burbling stream. Looking up, you see a hollow in front of you carpeted with soft, light green moss. A beam of sunlight illuminates the area, sparkling on a small, golden chest nestled in the moss.

Kneel down in the soft, dry moss and open the chest. Inside you will find a symbol, some sort of object that reminds you of your own personal value. It can be just one object or a collection of objects. Maybe it's a piece of parchment with something written on it; perhaps it's a ring or a collection of coins. It can be anything that symbolizes to you a time or experience you can feel proud of—a time that makes you feel good about you.

One person might find a champagne glass from their wedding day. Another could find a checkbook, symbolizing financial success. The object can be a flower from the garden you're proud of, a letter, a rock from the beach. Allow your unconscious mind to reveal to you the symbol that most represents one aspect of your value.

Do this exercise every day for a week, allowing yourself to find other symbolic objects. Embrace them as reminders to yourself of your inherent goodness and worth. You can return to this exercise anytime you are having feelings of low self-esteem.

Your Inner Guide

· · · · · · · · · · · ·

Sometimes, when you feel a little low or lost, you may wish you knew someone very wise, someone who could help you feel better. As a matter of fact, you do know someone that wise—*yourself*. In truth, no one knows more about you than you do. And while that wisdom is sometimes hidden—even unconscious—it's there if you have techniques to access it.

An easy way to contact your acquired wisdom is to imagine an inner guide—an embodiment of your deepest knowledge about yourself, a being who can clarify your feelings and show you a path to self-acceptance. Your inner guide can take the shape of a deceased parent, a long-lost friend or teacher, a character from a book or movie, or even an animal.

You can consciously decide on an inner guide, or you can wait and see what kind of figure your subconscious mind dreams up during the exercise that follows. One caution before you try this exercise: If at any time you feel uncomfortable or think the guide that is emerging is scary or threatening, stop the visualization and try again later. Wait until you are in a frame of mind that allows you to conjure up a pleasant, warm, safe, and supportive guide.

Now, close your eyes and imagine hearing a doorbell. See yourself walking slowly and calmly toward the sound of the bell. You approach a large door made of smoked glass and backed by a screen door. Through the door you begin to be able to see the outline of your guide. Notice the physical details of your inner guide: short or tall? thin or heavy?

Unlock and open the glass door, leaving the screen closed. You can see all of your guide through the screen, although he or she looks a little shadowy. Look carefully now and see the details of your guide's appearance. Is it someone you know? Someone you've read about or seen in a movie? Maybe your guide is a combination of people you have known.

When you are comfortable with your guide, open the screen door and invite him or her to come in and sit down. Smile, and see your guide smile back. Shake hands, touch, or hug if that feels right.

Ask your guide, "Are you willing to help me?" and wait for an answer. Your guide may respond with words or gestures, or you may just sense an answer.

Now ask your guide, "How can I appreciate myself? How can I find the good within me?" Accept whatever response is made, without judgment. You may have to imagine your guide several times before you start getting clear answers.

You can consult your guide anytime, about anything—problems you're having, things that are worrying you, decisions you have to make, or things in your life that are unclear. You may be surprised at the clarity and simplicity of the replies.

When you are done, say good-bye to your guide and allow him or her to leave. Remember that your guide can visit you whenever you need a reminder of your worth or help deciding on a path.

Self-Worth Visualization

. . . .

Your mind and body will respond the same way to imaginary experiences as to real ones. For example, if you can see yourself feeling good and acting freely at a party, you will get almost the same kind of confidence—equal to actually going to the party and successfully interacting. Visualization is a powerful method of reprogramming the ways you think and react.

You can use visualization to create scenes in your head in which your behavior shows you're worthy instead of unworthy, confident instead of doubtful, attractive instead of ugly. Begin by retiring to a quiet place and relaxing. With your eyes closed, breathing slowly and deeply, imagine this scene:

You are taking a bath. There is soothing music playing and you are relaxed and smiling. The warm water glides over your limbs, and you can smell the lavender-scented soap. You feel invigorated and calm.

Now you're out of the bath and dried off. You're slipping into comfortable, loose clothing and you look in the mirror. Instead of chastising yourself and focusing on the areas you don't like, you admire the shape of your eyes or the softness of your skin. You might notice the way your damp hair clings to your neck, the sensuous look in your eyes after soaking in the bath, or the strength and definition of your muscles. Tell yourself, "I feel good, and I look how I feel—secure and beautiful."

If you feel yourself automatically starting to criticize something about your looks, stop yourself and refocus. Recall a compliment someone has paid you in the past—notice features that are uniquely yours, that make you who you are.

Now imagine entering the kitchen and preparing something delicious and healthy that will make you feel energetic. Take the time to enjoy the colors or to arrange your food attractively on the plate. Tell yourself, "I deserve to eat and feel well."

Now imagine walking down the street. You pass a stranger. Tell yourself, "I am willing to take risks." Imagine yourself smiling, with the same emotions you felt in your warm, comfortable bath. The stranger makes eye contact and smiles back. You feel a rush of confidence and pleasure.

Get ready to end this session. When you are ready to go about your daily routine, recall this visualization and repeat your statements to yourself, such as "I feel good and I look how I feel—secure and beautiful," or "I am willing to take risks." Keep this exercise up, imagining different scenes, and notice the gradual difference in your feelings of worth and confidence.

Hypnosis for Self-Esteem

. . . .

A group of friends gathered in the living room after dinner to play a parlor game where each would confess something they had never told anybody. A woman revealed that her mother's nickname for her as a child was "Duh-duh." "I used to say 'Duh,' when I was a baby, which she thought was funny, because she didn't think I was very smart. And I guess for as long as I can remember I thought that too."

When core beliefs about self-esteem are developed at an early age, you may need special techniques to change them. Hypnosis is a powerful tool for revising early parental programming.

The affirmation "I am a kind and generous person" is helpful when repeated throughout the day. But the same suggestion offered during hypnosis can change at the deepest level negative parental messages.

Rest your elbow on a table or the arm of a chair. Let your hand dangle over the edge with a pencil between your thumb and index finger. The pencil should be suspended above the ground so that when it falls, you'll hear the noise. Get comfortable, close your eyes, and take a few slow, deep breaths. Tell yourself that when you're sufficiently relaxed, the pencil will slip out of your fingers and drop. That will be your sign to let go completely and drift into a deep state of relaxation.

While you're waiting for the pencil to drop, say these words to yourself: "I am drifting deeper and deeper, deeper and deeper . . . I am drifting down, down, down into total relaxation . . . I am drowsy and drifting, drifting and drowsy . . . I am more and more drowsy, peaceful, and calm." Just keep saying these same phrases over and over, mixing them in any order and taking deep, slow breaths until the pencil drops.

When you hear the pencil fall, say to yourself a preplanned affirmation of your strengths and worth. It could be as simple as "I am a good person." Or it could be more specific: "I am good and competent and careful in my work." However you phrase it, make it one clear, positive sentence. Slowly, silently repeat the affirmation three times.

Now make the following posthypnotic suggestion: "Today I like myself more than yesterday, and tomorrow I will like myself more than today. Tomorrow I will remember more and more of the good about myself." After making the suggestion, take several more deep breaths and tell yourself that you will become fully alert on the count of three. Count up slowly to three. Open your eyes, move around, and make sure you are wide awake.

This hypnosis exercise will put you into a mild trance that is perfectly safe (as long as you make sure you're fully alert before driving or using machinery) and should take no more than three minutes. Generally it is helpful to alternate your strengths affirmation, but you're encouraged to repeat affirmations that feel important to you as often as it feels helpful.

PART II

Conquer Your Inner Critic

Essential to understanding self-esteem is the concept of the Pathological Inner Critic. This is the name given to the "voice" we all hear in our heads from time to time, that critical monologue that reminds you of your weaknesses and failings. It may remind you of your own voice or of one of your parents' voices. It may consist of isolated words, brief mental images, or long diatribes. In any case, it is this inner critic who destroys self-esteem. This section will teach you how to identify your inner critic's messages, silence or refute them, and create an alternative, healthy, self-affirming voice of advocacy within yourself.

Meet Your Critic

. . . .

Don't worry if you hear voices inside your head. Everybody does. It's called *self-talk* or your *internal monologue*. It's the natural, everyday mental commentary that helps you interpret what's going on, avoid danger or pain, seek out pleasure or gain, and make choices and decisions.

Critical thinking is an essential faculty—you have to make critical judgments to survive. If you have low self-esteem, however, you apply too many critical judgments to yourself. They get out of control and take on a life of their own. This out-of-control critical voice in your head is called the *pathological critic*.

Your pathological critic is the negative inner voice that says, "I'm fat, I'm ugly, I'm incompetent." The critic blames you for things that go wrong. The critic compares you to others and finds you wanting. The critic expects you to be perfect, constantly reminding you of your weaknesses and failures but never once mentioning your strengths and successes. The critic reads your friends' minds and tells you they are bored and turned off by you. The critic makes absolute statements like "You always screw up, you *never* finish anything on time."

This voice may sound like a man or a woman, like your mother or your father, or like your own voice. For many people it doesn't sound like a separate voice at all—self-critical "truths" or "facts" just pop into their minds. That's a key feature of the pathological critic: No matter how outrageous its statements are, they seem true. You believe them without question.

To raise your self-esteem, you have to start noticing and questioning your pathological critic. To start with, think of the one negative truth about yourself—that is, something that you view as negative—that you believe without question. What is your major vice, weak point, disability, or lack—the one that is obvious to you and anyone who knows you? This can be something as obvious and factual as "I'm short," "I dropped out of high school," or "I'm single."

For the rest of the day, and all day tomorrow, simply notice how many times this fact enters your mind. Carry a pen and paper around and tally how many times you think about it. If you actually hear the words in your head, jot that down, too. It's good practice for later exercises.

But for now, just notice how much this fact is on your mind. Seems like a lot, doesn't it? That's the pathological critic, keeping the spotlight on the negative, constantly reminding you of your faults and misfortunes. Once you've observed how present the belief is in your life, you can move on to the other exercises in this section.

Catching Your Critic

· · · · · · · · · · · · · · · ·

You've seen it a hundred times in the movies: the CIA agents in the fake plumber's van, clutching their earphones, listening in on conversations being held over a tapped phone line; the private eye using the voice-activated tape recorder; the suspicious person picking up the extension to hear their partner planning a secret rendezvous with a lover.

Catching your critic is like being a detective. Only in this case, you are tapping into your own thoughts, monitoring your internal monologue for critical self-statements.

Carry a notebook with you tomorrow. As you go about your usual routine, imagine that you are a detective, staked out in a corner of your own mind. Imagine that you can listen in on your own train of thought, like listening in on someone else's phone conversation.

When your internal monologue becomes judgmental, jot down your critic's attacks. Here's a sample taken from the notebook of a first-grade teacher:

Time	Critical Statement
8:15 A.M.	I'm always late. Why can't I get here on time?
8:40 A.M.	What a skimpy lesson plan. God, I'm lazy.
9:45 A.M.	You're letting these kids down.
11:00 A.M.	Still haven't hung up their drawings. I'm so disorganized.
12:20 P.M.	Stupid remark in the lunchroom.
2:35 P.M.	You're letting these kids get out of control.

When you first try this, your internal detective will probably nod off right away. It's hard to stay detached enough from your own life so that you can monitor your thoughts. You might have to "rewind the tape" in order to notice what you have been saying to yourself. When you remember that you are supposed to be noticing your thoughts, start with whatever you just thought about and work backward.

For example, the teacher noticed a library book, and that reminded her that she was supposed to keep track of her negative thoughts. She worked backward: "I was thinking, 'I don't have time to return the library book because I need to talk to Barbara after school and explain what I meant about the science fair, because in the lunchroom I'm sure I wasn't clear and I must have sounded really stupid.' I should write down, 'Stupid remark in the lunchroom.' "

Keep doing this exercise until your detective can stay awake long enough or you can rewind the tapes well enough to write down what your critic says to you.

The Origin of the Critic

· · · · · · · · · · · · · ·

The pathological critic begins with your parents' *forbidding gestures*—their negative reactions, such as scolding or hitting—when you did something dangerous, wrong, or annoying. These forbidding gestures told you that you were bad, that there was something wrong with you. When you're a kid, your parents' disapproval is a life and death matter, since they are the sole source of physical and emotional nourishment.

You retain conscious and unconscious memories of all those times when you were punished and felt wrong or bad. These are the unavoidable scars that growing up inflicts on everyone's self-esteem. When your pathological critic starts pointing out how you've made a mess, fallen short of a goal, or made a stupid mistake, it sounds perfectly believable because it harks back to your earliest memories of punishment, shame, and fear.

The nastiness of your pathological critic depends on how frequent, rejecting, consistent, moralistic, and blaming your parents' forbidding gestures were. The more "yes" answers you make to the following five questions, the more likely you are to have a loud and vicious internal critic:

1. Did your parents scold or punish you frequently? _____ yes _____ no

    It takes many repetitions of "You always screw up. What's the matter with you?" before it sinks in and becomes part of your pathological critic's repertoire.

2. Did your parents reject you by anger or withdrawal? _____ yes _____ no

Children can tolerate a fair amount of criticism without damage to their sense of worth, if the criticism is delivered in a calm, supportive way. Damage is done when parents yell and hit or withdraw their emotional support.

3. **Did your parents have inconsistent rules?** _____ yes _____ no

When parents don't enforce the rules consistently, it makes it hard for you to figure out what is expected of you. When you're punished, you are more likely to assume it's because you're bad by nature, not just breaking a clear rule.

4. **Did your parents make everything a moral issue?** _____ yes _____ no

If your parents considered being noisy, getting a low grade, or breaking something a mortal sin, you are more likely to have low self-esteem than if they expressed their rules in terms of preferences, tastes, personal needs, or safety issues.

5. **Did your parents blame you rather than your behavior?** _____ yes _____ no

A child who hears a stern warning about the danger of running into the street will have better self-esteem than a child who only hears that she's a "bad girl" when she runs into the street. Careful parents make a clear distinction between their child's inappropriate behavior and the basic goodness of their child.

Your answers to these questions can help you identify the origins of your critic. It is important to remember that you can alter and control your critic, even if you answered yes to all of these questions. The following exercises in this section will help you do so.

Who's Afraid
of the Big Bad Critic?

· · · · · · · · · · · · ·

The pathological critic is not the bogeyman, a demon, an alien, or the big bad wolf. It is just a combination of all the negative voices you've heard over the years. It seems scary because it has been part of you for so long and it knows how to push your buttons.

You can overcome your fear of the critic the same way public speakers overcome their fear of the audience: imagine your critic naked. That is, imagine the critic as someone who is vulnerable, exposed, funny looking, ridiculous, and so on. This accomplishes two things. It exposes the ridiculous nature of much of what your critic says, and it makes it the "other," something outside of yourself that can be rejected without rejecting the essential you.

The next time you notice your critic yammering in your mind's ear, visualize it as someone silly or contemptible, someone on the outside of you whom you can easily dismiss. Here are some ways to see your critic that will make it less scary and easier to ignore:

- **Politician.** Imagine the stuffed shirt, windbag type of politician droning on about some stupid scheme that nobody in their right mind would take seriously. Hear your critic being hissed and booed from the podium.

- **Carney barker.** Imagine an old-fashioned sideshow barker in a cheap suit with bad teeth, trying to convince you to leave the sunlight and enter into a mildewed tent to admire a cloudy jar of formaldehyde not quite preserving what might once have been a two-headed rabbit. You find it easy to tune out your critic and walk on past.

- **Spokesmodel.** Imagine a bottle blonde grandly gesturing toward a toaster oven. You smile a pitying "No thanks."

- **Telemarketer.** Imagine a thrice-divorced lapsed scientologist in a dank studio apartment in Reno, Nevada, surrounded by pizza boxes, beanie babies, and pictures of Elvis, chain-smoking and drinking straight out of a two-liter bottle of diet soda, dialing you up to see if you'd like two free weeks of a newspaper you wouldn't use to line your birdcage. You gently hang up, unplug the cord from the wall, and run the whole phone through the trash compactor, just to be on the safe side.

- **Clown.** Imagine someone in a clown suit with a huge painted smile that doesn't hide the anxious grimace as he or she struggles to produce a series of balloon animals. "Voilà," the clown gasps. "A griffin . . . a dragon . . . a unicorn." They all look the same, like three-legged poodles with hip problems. As you walk by, you shift your bundles so that your hands are full and you don't have to take a malformed poodle.

- **Madman.** Imagine someone standing on the street corner wearing a sandwich board, explaining to the air that he or she is picking up radio waves containing Richard Nixon's plans for world domination, broadcast by aliens to the spy antennas the CIA installed in his or her teeth. You try not to make eye contact as you get the hell out of there.

Unmasking Your Critic

. . . .

Your critic pretends to be you, masquerading as the reciter of obvious of facts or the rational voice of planning or analysis. Your critic may pretend to have your best interests at heart. But it's a sham. Your critic lies. Your critic operates from motives that may seem reasonable on the surface, but they're actually harmful. You must strip the mask away and expose your critic's ulterior motives.

Continue to jot down messages from your critic (as discussed in previous exercises in this section). Study them to find a pattern. Which subjects and themes does your critic return to again and again? What is the tone of voice? What are your critic's favorite words and phrases?

Why does your critic do this to you? What are its motives? Why does it pick certain things to harp on? See if you can explain your critic's motivations to yourself. Write down "My critic . . . ," and spell out why your critic says what it says. Here are some ulterior motives that others have come up with:

- My critic tries to enforce the rules I grew up with because that's all it knows.

- My critic compares me to others because—once in a great while—I get to feel superior to somebody.

- My critic is believable because it sounds like my parents, and I always believed them.

- My critic kicks me around just like my parents did.

34

- My critic expects perfection because if I could just do everything right, I might feel okay about myself.

- My critic says I'm incompetent to keep me from trying—that way I won't have to feel bad about failing.

- My critic tells me people won't like me so I won't be so surprised and hurt when they reject me.

- My critic predicts the worst so I'll be prepared for it.

- My critic tells me to be perfect so that I can actually think I'm capable of perfection for at least one comforting moment.

- My critic tortures me so I can atone for past mistakes.

If any of these common ulterior motives are familiar, write down your own versions of them. Writing them out in full helps reveal how convoluted and illogical they are.

Notice that many of your critic's motives may be laudable, designed to save you pain in some roundabout way. But the motives are like left-handed compliments or consolation prizes—they hurt more than they help.

When you unmask your critic's motives, you make its criticisms less believable. You become less susceptible to your critic's ravings and more prepared to answer back with healthy self-statements that will increase your self-esteem.

Talking Back to
Your Critic with Mantras

● ● ● ● ● ● ● ● ● ● ● ● ● ● ● ●

The mantras recommended for this exercise aren't ones like "om" or "serenity." The ones discussed in this exercise are sometimes called the *blocking mantras*, because they answer your critic's sniping shots of negativity with a mental stop sign.

Blocking mantras are easy to use. When you notice that your critic is piping up with the usual "That was stupid" or "Nobody likes you," you respond by imagining shouting at the top of your voice. You silently yell, *"Shut up!"* or some other short, forceful expletive that can drown out your critic's voice. Here are some mantras that have worked for others:

This is poison! Stop it!

Shut up, liar!

Cut this crap!

Screw you, critic!

To hell with these put-downs!

Get off my back!

It's perfectly all right to swear at your critic. You can rant and rave in your mind. You don't have to be nice or logical. In fact, you don't even have to make sense. For example, Leslie's critic often spoke with her mother's voice, reciting long strings of warnings and advice: "Watch out . . . be careful, you'll drop it . . . you're so clumsy . . . everyone can see you're a klutz . . . stand up straight, you look like a pretzel." Leslie found that the most effective mantra was the one she had discovered at age six, after seeing *Mary Poppins*. When her mother was berating her, the six-year old Leslie kept repeating "Supercalifragilistic-expialidocious!" over and over, at the top of her voice, until her mother finally stopped. What worked then works now. Leslie says the nonsense word in her mind at top volume, and by the second or third repetition, her critic's tapes shut off.

What would you like to say to your harshest critics, especially your internal critic? Write down at least three possible mantras here and practice them over the next week.

_____

_____

_____

_____

If you want to increase your mantra's effectiveness, put a rubber band around one wrist. When shouting your mantra in your mind, reach over and snap the rubber band against your wrist. The sharp, stinging sensation breaks the train of negative self-talk and acts as a minor punishment, which makes your critic a little less likely to attack the next time. Think of the rubber band snap as a physiological exclamation point added to the end of your internal mantra.

Try this exercise for a week, whenever you notice your critic's comments. Try many mantras and continue the ones you like the best after the week is complete. And remember, the critic never shuts up for good, so use your mantras whenever they're needed.

Remind Your Critic of the Cost

• • • • • • • • • • • • • • • • • •

Your pathological critic is like a compulsive gambler: it spends all your emotional capital to pay off the loan shark of the past. The truth is, you don't owe the past anything. Your critic costs you way more than it affords. You can remind it of that cost and refuse to pay.

What is the "cost" of a noisy critic in terms of self-esteem? You can't lay out the dollars and cents in a ledger, but you can list the problems in your life that low self-esteem causes or makes worse. Here's a list of "costs" for Lorraine, a sales rep for a printing company:

- I'm overly defensive when my husband criticizes me.

- I blow up at my son when he defies me.

- I lost Eileen as a friend when I got so angry.

- I snap at my mother whenever she makes suggestions about money.

- I'm not assertive enough with clients.

- I'm cold and distant with bosses because I fear them.

- I feel anxious and on guard around strangers.

- I assume people won't like me.

- I'm afraid to try new things for fear of looking stupid.

When Lorraine saw how much poor self-esteem was costing her, she wrote out a succinct statement to remind her critic of the cost: "You make me defensive and afraid of people, you cut my income, you lose me friends, and you make me mean to the people I love."

Write down what low self-esteem costs you in these areas:

Intimate relationships _____

Relatives _____

Work _____

Meeting new people _____

Trying new things _____

Others _____

_____

Now combine the most important items into a summary statement and write it in the space provided.

I can't afford this. You've cost me _____

_____

Whenever your critic attacks, you can fight back using this phrase.

Talking Back by Affirming Your Worth

· · · · · · · · · · · · · ·

While talking back to your critic with mantras and reminding your critic of the cost of its tirades are important, these methods are insufficient in the long run. They are techniques that give you practice in responding to your critic and buy you time—but they don't solve the problem itself. In the end, all they amount to is "Shut up" and "I can't afford it." If you've ever been called repeatedly by a telemarketer, you know these strategies won't work forever. Especially since your critic is the telemarketer from hell, with vast knowledge of your vulnerabilities and a direct line to your mind—and you have no way to hang up.

The weakness of "Shut up" and "I can't afford it" is that they create a vacuum by silencing the critic—without putting anything in its place. Soon enough your critic's voice will be back, filling the vacuum with more attacks. You need to fill that vacuum with positive awareness of your own worth. That isn't easy, since up until now you have sincerely agreed with your critic that there is something fundamentally wrong with you.

Your critic would have you believe that you are a worthless, empty vessel that must be filled up, drop by drop, with your accomplishments. According to this view, everybody starts out essentially worthless, a body that moves and talks. The critic claims that there is no *intrinsic* value in a person, only a *potential* for doing something worthwhile, something important.

That's a lie. The truth is that you are a precious and unique vessel, regardless of "contents." Just consider how parents adore their newborns, full of love and wonder for little beings who can't even focus their eyes, let alone talk, and haven't accomplished a thing yet.

The truth is that your value is your consciousness, your aliveness, your ability to perceive and experience. The value of a human life is that it exists. You are a complex miracle of creation. You are a person who is trying to live, and that makes you as worthwhile as every other person who is doing the very same thing. Daily achievements have nothing to do with your intrinsic value.

When your critic starts harassing you about your shortcomings, your emptiness, and your lack of accomplishments when compared with others, you need to answer back with affirmations of your essential worth. Here are some examples that have worked for others:

- I am worthwhile because I live and breathe and feel.

- I'm doing the best I can to survive. There's no need to beat myself up.

- I'm as good as anybody. We're all trying to survive on this planet.

- I love, I suffer, I struggle just like everyone else.

Try these out in your own mind. If none of them feel right, take a moment to write down an affirmation in your own words that sounds better to you.

Use these affirmations whenever your critic acts up and it seems the most appealing among the various techniques. When affirmations are effective, you won't hear from your critic for longer intervals of time, and when it does say something, it will be at a much lower volume.

Your Advocate's Voice

· · · · · · · · · · · · · · · ·

Monday morning, Sally woke up and turned sleepily to look over at the brand-new dress, pair of tights, and shoes resting on her bureau. She had bought them over the weekend, and she was really looking forward to wearing them that day. It made Monday so much brighter when she had something new to wear.

She got to work, smiled at the receptionist, Maurice, and made her way to her office. "Hmm," Sally thought to herself. "I guess Maurice didn't notice the dress. Oh well." Trouble was, throughout the rest of the day, no one seemed to notice Sally's new ensemble. She became convinced that no one mentioned her new clothes because the outfit was really wrong and everyone was simply too embarrassed to say it. "I have horrible taste!" Sally thought.

Sally went through the last half of her day feeling miserable. By the time she got to her dinner date with her best friend, Bernice, she was full of apologies. "Sorry I'm not looking my best. I don't know what possessed me to buy this dress—I must be blind." Sally slumped into her chair and took a slug of Bernice's wine. "You must be joking," Bernice retorted. "I love your taste in clothes! What great adventurousness. You look fantastic!"

Bernice wouldn't hear of Sally putting herself down. As a good friend, she sees Sally with the kind of love that Sally, with all of her negative self-talk, sometimes has trouble feeling for herself. If only Bernice were inside Sally's head, nipping those negative statements in the bud!

The following exercise will allow you to imagine a good friend's voice fighting your pathological critic. After practice, your friend's voice of love and support will meld with your own inner voice, combating your critic's attacks.

For one whole day, keep track of all of your negative self-talk. When you catch your critic sniping at you, take a moment and write down those negative statements. Don't judge them at this point—just write them all down.

At the end of the day, examine the list of your critic's negative statements. Now, imagine that you are your strongest advocate—maybe it's your best friend, a parent, or a mentor. Choose someone you know who'd defend you against the emotional grenades your critic throws your way, and try to put yourself inside your advocate's head. On a separate sheet of paper, rebut each negative self-statement. For example, if your critical inner voice said, "You're so disorganized!" your advocate might respond by saying, "Sometimes your creative nature prevents you from being perfectly organized." If your critic told you, "You always say the stupidest things," your friend might say, "I love your stories. They're so funny and unique!"

Now, go through your advocate's rebuttals and let your critic respond to each of your advocate's positive points about you. Then, let your advocate speak to these new criticisms. Your advocate should respond cordially but firmly in your favor. If your critic responds to your advocate complimenting your creativity with "You may be creative, but your office is a pigsty," your advocate might say, "Living a rich, creative life is much more important to you than always being tidy." If your critic doesn't buy that your stories are funny and says, "You try so hard to be funny that other people think you're a show-off," your friend's voice could say, "People enjoy your stories. If they thought you were showing off, they wouldn't listen and laugh when you talk."

Continue this process, letting your critic respond to the advocate's points until it runs out of steam. In the face of a steadfastly positive advocate, the critic will run out of criticisms. And, at the end of the exercise, you'll have a list of positive statements that you can use to remind yourself of your wonderful qualities. You can repeat this exercise whenever new criticisms, or variations of old ones, pop up in your mind.

The Critic's Favorite Attack: Negative Comparisons

• • • • • • • • • • • • • • • •

Sandra tore away at her thumbnail as she waited for class to begin. Her friend, Elise, sat beside her, drumming her fingers against the armrest. They were both feeling a little tense because they were due to get their midterm papers back, and their professor was a notoriously tough grader.

Finally the professor walked in and immediately began to return the papers. The closer the professor got, the more vigorously Sandra chewed and Elise tapped. Just as Sandra managed to rip the nail below the quick, her paper slid onto her desk. A big red B stared up at her. "What a bummer!" Sandra thought to herself. "I worked harder on this paper than I ever have before. I thought for sure I'd get an A this time."

Sandra turned to give a sad half-smile to Elise—who was smiling broadly. Sandra looked at Elise's paper—A+! "Wow! That's great, Elise." She patted Elise on the back and surreptitiously slid her other hand over her B. She could never do as well as Elise on term papers. Sandra figured she was just a lousy writer. A pretty rotten student, for that matter. Disorganized, slow, lazy . . .

Sandra feels bad that she didn't do as well as Elise on the paper, but she's sliding into a total negation of her skills as a student because of one less-than-sterling grade. Sandra is seeing things through the gloomy filter of her low self-esteem. She forgets that she's terrific in French, that she aced her math quiz, that her friends love her sense of humor, that she can make a mean soufflé. Everything gets reduced to one negative comparison.

The following exercise will help you learn to cut yourself a break when faced with negative comparison. Everyone is good in varying degrees at different things. Here's a way to honor what *you* do well.

For the rest of today and all day tomorrow, make a note every time you compare yourself negatively to someone else. Use a pad of paper or a journal, and the next time you notice how much better someone else is at something, write it down ("10:34 A.M.—Noticed how much better Bob is at speaking in the staff meeting").

At the end of the day, go through your list. Consider each negative comparison carefully. Then, for each one, think of something that *you* do better than the other person. Write it down beside the negative comparison. The thing you're more successful at can be anything that's important to you—maybe you get along with people better than Susan, or you're a nattier dresser than Walter. Perhaps you write better than Joe, or you can tell a funnier story than Clarise. Whatever it is, don't be shy about acknowledging it and writing it on your list.

As a final step, take a good look at the list you've created. Think about how you felt when you wrote the first negative comparison. Then, note how you feel when you realize that there are plenty of things that you do well, too—even things that you do much *better* than other people. Tomorrow, when you find yourself comparing yourself negatively to someone else, take the opportunity to consider what you might do better than that person. Practice throughout the day.

Repeat this exercise daily for a week or two, and then repeat it whenever negative comparisons come up again. If the exercise is successful, you will find yourself making fewer negative comparisons as time passes.

Letters to Your Critical Parent

· · · · · · · · · · · · · · · · · · ·

For many people, the critic's voice sounds a lot like a parent's voice. In fact, you may be able to trace your struggles with self-esteem back to a particularly critical, angry, or neglectful parent.

If you have feelings of anger and disappointment that you could never adequately express to your parent, this exercise can be especially helpful. It will allow you to express all those feelings you never could before, as well as help you put yourself in your parent's shoes. In a small way, you'll get a chance to "reparent" yourself through the medium of writing.

You will be writing three letters: the first to your critical parent, the second *as* your critical parent, and the third as the parent you wish you'd had.

To begin, write a letter to the parent that disappointed you. Whether he or she was overly critical, angry, absent, or ineffectual, you needed something else from them—and you didn't get it. In this first letter, tell your parent exactly what you needed and how it felt not to get it.

Dolores, a thirty-year-old woman who is full of self-doubt, started her letter this way:

I need to tell you that you didn't give me the support and attention I needed from you. You hurt me by not being there, and by putting me down when you were. The wounds remain. Because you never, ever acknowledged my fundamental worth, I still question it today.

Your second letter will be in your parent's voice. How would this parent *realistically* respond to what you wrote? Would he or she understand? Would your parent be defensive or angry? Would he or she make an effort to accept your feelings? Use your imagination and your powers of empathy to put yourself into that parent's shoes and write a response in his or her voice.

Dolores wrote a response that included both defensiveness and understanding:

I never wanted to criticize you, but sometimes you needed it. Life is hard, and you needed to toughen up to survive. Look at me: I had to work two jobs to support you, and no one was giving me a break. I gave you as much time as I had. You need to get over that. But I'm sorry I hurt you.

Your final letter will be in the voice of the parent you wished you'd had—the parent you needed. In this letter, you will, through your ideal parent's voice, remind yourself that you *deserved* to get whatever you needed as a child. Anything that held your parent back from giving you what you needed was that parent's problem, and at its root it had nothing to do with you or your worth as a person.

Dolores's ideal parent wrote this:

I'm truly sorry that I was unable to give you everything you really needed as a child. I guess I could never acknowledge what a treasure you were to me or how very proud I am of you. That's because I never learned how to express my loving feelings without shame. And, even though this is my deficit and had nothing to do with you, you suffered from it. Please accept my apology and know that you are supremely valuable to me. I love you and I think you've become an exceptional adult.

Dolores found that even months after she wrote her letters, phrases from her ideal parent's letter came to mind during stressful times, helping her to cope without beating up on herself.

PART III

Refute Self-Esteem Wreckers

Self-esteem wreckers are the tools your pathological critic employs to demolish your self-worth. They are the habits of thought that you consistently use to interpret reality, such as overgeneralization or global labeling. Fortunately, self-esteem wreckers are only a bad habit, and habits can be broken. You can learn to refute each self-esteem wrecker and feel better about yourself.

Self-esteem wreckers can be tricky to pinpoint at first, because they are part of how you perceive reality. As you read this section, you will likely find that there are some self-esteem wreckers that you identify more with—focusing on the exercises for those particular self-esteem wreckers will help you demolish them. Once you've identified your self-esteem wreckers and have committed yourself to overcoming self-attacking thoughts, you can begin to develop effective rebuttals to your self-esteem wreckers. It can help to imagine a specific person as your rebuttal voice—someone who can stand up to your self-esteem wrecker when you're down. This person becomes the champion of your cause, your advisor, teacher, or coach. Imagine an accepting friend, for example, who is totally on your side. He or she would remind you of your good points when you forget them. Or imagine a rational teacher who is stern but kind—he or she will point out opportunities to learn or grow.

As you go through the process of combating your self-esteem wreckers, remember that your thoughts determine your feelings. Your self-esteem wreckers are only a bad habit—a habit of thought and a way of interpreting reality that makes you feel bad about yourself. Once you know some of your wrecker thoughts, you can begin to combat them.

Overgeneralization

· · · · · · · · · · · ·

Overgeneralization creates a shrinking universe in which more and more absolute conclusions make life increasingly confining. Instead of observing all available data, formulating a conclusion that explains all of the data, and then testing the conclusion, you take one fact or event, make a general rule out of it, and never test out the rule. If you have a tendency to overgeneralize, you may interpret one bad experience at an Italian restaurant to mean that all Italian food is bad.

Clues that you are overgeneralizing are words like *never, all, every, everyone, nobody,* or *always.* These kinds of absolute words are your critic's way of closing the door of possibility, inhibiting your access to change or growth. Read the following example to see if you suffer from the same self-esteem wrecker as Annie.

Annie, age twenty-five, has a terrible fear of making the "first move" while on a date. Her fear has become so great that she is beginning to wonder if she'll ever feel confident again. She has felt this way since she was seventeen and she had her first date with Stu, her humorous and attractive lab partner in biology.

Stu and Annie often found themselves giggling quietly together during the many grue-some dissections they carried out as a team. She never thought she could have so much fun pinning down an earthworm. Annie was usually pretty shy about laughing and exposing her braces, but with Stu, she found herself letting go of some of her inhibitions.

One day after lab, they decided they should get together later that night and see a movie. Annie was jittery with anticipation. But once they were actually hanging out, she felt more at ease. In fact, by the end of the night, Annie had had such a good time that she was even feeling rather brave. While Stu was bent over tying his shoe, she decided she would plant a big kiss right on Stu's cheek as he came back up to face her. But Stu stood up just a tad bit quicker than Annie was moving. Her kiss ended up being a slightly open-mouthed attack on his nose, her braces gashing his tender cartilage, bringing bright red blood to the surface as evidence of her bungled maneuver.

Stu grabbed his mangled face and, grimacing in pain, said, "Jesus, what'd ya think I was, one of our lab animals? I'd better stick to dating girls on my swim team."

Annie was horrified and didn't realize Stu was over his shock by the next day. It was too late for Annie; she was scarred by the experience.

Ever since her date with Stu, she has been sure she is incapable of a graceful first move. Annie became so convinced of her incompetence that she began to even avoid eye contact at those particular moments on a date that can invite a possible kiss. This led to a generalized fear of dating, and Annie found herself thinking that she would *never* feel comfortable, that she would *always* be alone. She allowed this one negative experience to become a self-esteem wrecker. Luckily, her fear was based on overgeneralizing, a habit that she can break!

Annie needs to recognize her key words, such as *never, everyone,* and *always.* These are words that can alert her to the fact that her pathological critic is confining her with absolutes. Without taking risks and challenging these erroneous, absolute conclusions, Annie can never find the truth.

Is overgeneralization one of your self-esteem wreckers? Do you make broad, sweeping conclusions based on scanty evidence. Do you notice yourself saying or thinking statements that contain words like *all, every, always,* and *never,* or thinking things like, "Nobody loves me"?

You can beat this wrecker by softening the absolutes, looking for accurate descriptions rather than broad generalizations, and being as specific as possible with each individual incident.

How can you soften your absolutes? Well, first, try to second-guess them and look for *specific* clues in a situation. For instance, suppose you enjoy your co-workers, but feel left out because they don't invite you to lunch with them. If you're falling into the trap of overgeneralization, you immediately think, "*Nobody* likes me here. I'll *never* have any friends at this place." Write down the absolute words you are using and then check for evidence.

Then ask yourself, "What evidence do I have for these absolute conclusions?" Look for exceptions. Use more accurate words like *some, few,* and *once in a while.* For example, "A few people here may like me. Beth often asks me if I've read any good books lately. Bill offered to drive me to my car last night. And maybe some of my co-workers could be friends if I tried to approach *them*."

As you challenge these generalizations, you will see possibilities and options opening up for yourself.

Polarized Thinking

· · · · · · · · · · · ·

With this self-esteem wrecker, there are always only two choices: white or black; right or wrong. You insist on either/or choices, perceiving everything and everybody at the extremes—leaving very little room for a middle ground. Other people are either amazing or worthless, exciting or boring. If you get a speeding ticket, you're a lousy driver. If a friend doesn't return your call, they're undependable.

The real danger of this kind of thinking is that ultimately you're going to judge yourself according to these unrealistic standards, and it's impossible to live up to them. There's no room for mistakes.

Lucy, for example, believed that people who expressed anger and yelled were "out of control" and "horrible." She thought that everyone should be able to maintain their composure and that staying calm meant you were a "good" person. She could often hear her upstairs neighbors fighting, which convinced her that they were frightening people. She would suck in her breath with fear when she stood next to either of them at the apartment building mailboxes.

One day Lucy turned her car over to the valet-parking attendant while she did her Christmas shopping. Crazy last-minute shoppers terrorized the stores, each other, and Lucy. She tried to keep her cool and move along. People cut in front of her and stole the sale items from her hands while her head was turned, and someone even elbowed her in the gut, never stopping to apologize. But Lucy kept on trucking, occasionally biting her lower lip.

She kept her composure, that is, until she returned to the parking garage, when she discovered that the valet had rammed into her car door with another person's minivan. Lucy lost it. Her eyebrows came together in a fixed **V** and her face turned bright red. She laid into the kid with the red jacket who had been responsible for her car. She called him a good-for-nothing louse of an employee, among other things.

Lucy drove home in her car with the smashed door and shook with disdain for herself. She felt like such a failure—she was suddenly one of them, the angry, wicked, out-of-control people. Poor Lucy was so judgmental of normal human reactions that even she couldn't escape condemnation. She couldn't see that she had simply overreacted and that, even at the moment she exploded, she was still a generally good person.

The key to overcoming polarized thinking is to stop making black-or-white judgments. People are not either happy or sad, loving or rejecting, courageous or wimpy. They fall somewhere along a continuum. Humans are just too complex to be rigidly divided in this way.

If you make black-and-white judgments or see everything as awful or great—with no middle ground—you're probably being too hard on yourself and others. To combat polarized thinking, use precise descriptions, think in percentages, and look for and describe gray areas. For example, Lucy could have thought, "I was angry at that parking attendant and I took it out on him. Even though I said some unfair things, at the time I was being about 25 percent inappropriate and 75 percent appropriate. And the parking attendant's nonchalant attitude about the damage he had done made it even more difficult for me not to express my anger."

Instead of thinking about life in black and white, describe the specific shades of gray. For example, suppose you host a party and go to bed thinking, "What a complete flop! Everyone had a horrible time and went home early." Instead, be accurate, and think in percentages: "Nothing is so absolute. Even though 70 percent of my guests left early, there were at least 30 percent of my guests who stayed until almost 2 A.M., and we were all engaged in a really interesting conversation."

Filtering

. . . .

Do you ever feel that all you hear is the negative stuff? This can be a real self-esteem wrecker. You can only hear and see certain things, such as mistakes, rejection, loss, and so on. It's as if your eyes and ears literally have a filter on them, allowing the bad things to come through and keeping the good things out of your awareness. It's like pouring fresh-squeezed orange juice through a strainer and just keeping the pulp.

If, in many situations, you find evidence for your flaws, failures, and inadequacies, while taking little notice of your strengths or achievements, filtering may be one of your self-esteem wreckers. Suppose you prepared a dinner for friends, and everyone said how much they enjoyed it, but your brother mentioned that the soup was a bit salty— and all you end up remembering of the evening is that you oversalted the food. This is an example of filtering.

Carolyn, for instance, decided to take up mountain biking. Her best friend, Monique, was very experienced and offered to take her out and show her some tips. Monique praised Carolyn throughout their ride, commenting on her endurance and speed. Carolyn tried things she'd really never thought she'd have the guts to do, like riding alongside a cliff that promised a gruesome death if she made a wrong move, and watching her knuckles turn white from clinging to the handlebars as she pummeled down over roots and rocks.

At the end of the ride Monique mentioned that Carolyn might want to consider riding on her own a little in order to build up her confidence so that she could ride some of the more frightening terrain. Carolyn looked at her friend in horror, thinking, "You thought I wasn't taking enough risks? If that was easy, I must be the most unnatural bike rider ever. I must really suck, because I thought I was going to die out there!" She went home determined never to ride again, convinced she had proven herself to be the world's biggest wimp.

Carolyn was focusing only on Monique's negative comments and magnifying them as the whole truth. She forgot all of Monique's praise and encouragement. It's important to strive for a sense of balance if this is your self-esteem wrecker—you need to learn to see the negative comments in proportion to the rest of the feedback. You still have worth and value even if someone sees room for improvement!

If you struggle with *filtering*, focusing only on your mistakes, flaws, and failures, you need to shift your focus and look for some balancing, positive reality in a situation.

Global Labeling

• • • • • • • • • •

Global labeling is the self-esteem wrecker that will often cast you in the role of the simpleton or the villain. People who practice global labeling apply stereotyped labels to whole groups of people, things, behaviors, and experiences, as well as to themselves. It is closely related to overgeneralization, but instead of creating a rule you create a label. The labels usually include pejorative words, so pay attention if you are using negative descriptions of your appearance, performance, intelligence, and so on: "My love life is a total mess," "I'm just a failure, or "I'm neurotic."

Judy, for example, was quick to label herself thoughtless and selfish. She was so used to viewing herself in this light that she lost sight of the fact that she was actually a compassionate and kind friend to most people.

Most of Judy's immediate family lived in Chicago, and she lived in New York. Their relationship was based on phone conversations and e-mail, consisting of quick updates on each other. Judy received most of her information about her two older brothers, who still lived in Chicago, from her parents. Judy had a lot of admiration for her brothers but felt like she was the last one to be informed of major happenings in their lives. Although she felt left out, she blamed herself, thinking that she was the "bad" sister who moved away and deserved to be cut out of family news.

On one particular Christmas, Judy called home to wish everyone a happy holiday. Both of the brothers were there and took turns talking with her on the phone. They laughed and exchanged stories about the office, people they were dating, and movies. She hung up feeling close to them and not quite as guilty for moving away. However, she did have her usual pang that night as she was falling asleep, telling herself that she was selfish for having left her family to pursue her career in New York.

The next morning she got a call from her mother, who told her that her brother Rob had fallen asleep with a cigarette burning and had burned half of the house down. Judy felt horrible for her brother, knowing that he must be feeling guilty, and even worse for her parents, whose house had been seriously damaged. Judy was consumed with guilt. The tragedy made her feel even more distant.

She called Rob to see how he was handling the situation. His voice was cold and distant—he wouldn't even admit he felt guilty. He insisted that their parents had good insurance and that it wouldn't be that big of a deal. All Judy could think was, "Rob can't talk to me because he doesn't feel close to me! He thinks I moved away because I don't care. And it must be true—I am an egocentric person who doesn't care enough about her own family."

Judy was labeling herself based on the part of herself that was independent, not necessarily even selfish. But she focused on the global labels, using pejorative comments to describe her entire personality: She was *thoughtless* for moving away. She was *selfish* because she wasn't there for her family when something terrible happened.

When you struggle with global labeling, you find yourself using broad, negative labels like *stupid, selfish, ugly, weak, clumsy, failure, total loss*, and so on. Even verbs can function as global labels: *to lose, to fail, to waste*, or *to disgust*. When fighting global labels, you need to be specific and realize that your label is only referring to a *part* of you or an experience. If you look in the mirror and all you see is an overweight, *ugly* person, take a second look. Think to yourself: "Wait a minute. Let me be more precise—that's not me, that's just a label. What about the compliments I get on my shiny, healthy hair? And what about my rather unusual shade of greenish brown eyes? What about my strong chin? Maybe I'm fifteen pounds over my ideal, but my weight is only one aspect of my appearance."

Mind Reading

• • • • • • • • • • •

Mind reading is a self-esteem wrecker that assumes everyone thinks in the same way that you do. It's actually an easy habit to fall into, since it's based on projection—the belief that others share your negative opinions about yourself.

Take Maria, for example. Her boyfriend held a stressful job in the local fish market. Sam spent most of his day screaming orders at the top of his lungs to customers as buses and tourists whizzed past. He would come home at night with one goal: relaxation. Maria, on the other hand, worked as a park ranger and spent most of her days in quiet discussions with the furry creatures of the forest, who were not usually inclined to show a lot of interest in her ramblings.

Maria would come home at night ready to share her day with Sam. She wanted to tell him how much she hated the slobs who littered the campsites, the teenagers who left fast-food wrappers and beer cans throughout the park, and also how much she loved the changing colors of the trees and witnessing the first steps of a baby fawn. Sam would listen, quietly, with only a couple of words in response. Sometimes he would close his eyes and imagine the forest.

Maria, who already believed she was boring, would mind read that Sam felt she was boring too. When she saw Sam's eyes close, she became angry and would cut her story short. And she never thought to question it. Maria's conclusion was logical, but not accurate. She imagined that Sam saw her through the same dark lens through which she saw herself.

Mind reading is dangerous because the flaws you hate in yourself are rarely as big of a deal to others. Often they are invisible. The truth is, you are probably better off making no inferences about people's attitudes toward you. Assume nothing and keep a strictly open mind until some real evidence comes your way in the form of their words to you. Try to remind yourself that your notions about people are only hypotheses that need to be tested—by asking them. Directly checking out your mind-reading assumptions can protect you from some big blows to your self-esteem.

As Maria noticed Sam's eyes closing, she could have asked him what was going on with him. If only she had known how much he enjoyed the forest as she described it. By trying to read his mind instead of communicating, Maria ended up needlessly feeling hurt.

Mind reading occurs when you assume you know what others are thinking and feeling. If someone says or does something that makes you believe they think ill of you, force yourself to objectively look at the evidence. What, if anything, has the person told you directly? Suppose, for example, you've erroneously interpreted your mother-in-law's actions toward you to mean that she doesn't approve of your marrying her son or daughter. Although this may seem to be true—judging from the way she often speaks to you in a brusque manner—you still need to make a mental list of possible alternative interpretations. Find a way to check out your concerns. Use questions such as "I've had the feeling that you may be unhappy with me in some way. Is there anything to that?"

Remember—don't assume anything. When you catch yourself mind reading, it is important that you check for evidence, list alternative interpretations, and then check it out directly with the other person.

Shoulds

· · · · · · ·

Do you feel that you should have better self-confidence; that you should feel comfortable around others at all times; or that you should be the perfect lover, friend, or worker? If this sounds familiar, you may be plagued by the *should* self-esteem wrecker.

In this pattern, you have a list of strict rules—any deviation is *wrong*. And when you fail to live up to all the things you expect of yourself, it clobbers your sense of worth.

Take Jane, for example. This year, Jane was in charge of her company's annual holiday party. The first five years she'd worked with her company, she'd witnessed the office manager scrounging together odds and ends at the last minute and throwing some half-assed party (in the office, no less). In her assessment, the food was lousy, the music embarrassing, and the decorations "el cheapo."

Finally, Jane volunteered to take over the job. She had a vision of how everything *should* go. Two weeks before the party, she began organizing. She sent out memos asking everyone to bring a specific dish. This way, the menu would be perfectly balanced between dinner treats and sweets. She forgot about the alcohol, not being a drinker herself. She also called the local community hall to book a reservation, but they were already taken. Despite the fact that she felt the party should be outside of the office, Jane conceded to herself that she had no other choice. Besides, she consoled herself, at least everything else would be perfect.

Of course, things didn't work out as Jane had envisioned. The people who were assigned the dessert treats didn't show up, leaving the holiday party sugarless. And, since Jane had overlooked the alcohol, there were no party libations. The employees began going home after a half hour of tofu salad and mineral water.

Jane suddenly realized what a flop her party had turned out to be. She spent the rest of the evening in quiet desperation, counting the minutes until she could get into her car and escape. Her shoulds thundered down on her. "You should have planned better. You should have polled people for what they wanted. You should have kept out of it to begin with."

Jane's rigid expectations of what the holiday party should have been, what the office manager should have created in previous years, and how she should have organized the party this year led her into a trap. To combat this pattern of shoulds, Jane needs to reexamine her rules about the way things should be and learn to be more flexible.

Like Jane, you may have shoulds that make you despise yourself when you can't live up to them. The answer is to examine each strong should to see if it is sufficiently flexible and realistic. It's also important to assess if a should reflects your genuine, deeply held values, or whether it is a belief that's been pushed on you by family or friends. Ask yourself, "Given who I am and how I live, is this should helping or hurting me?"

Think of a specific should that's been coming up for you lately. Then, to combat this self-esteem wrecker, ask yourself if you can be more flexible. Ask yourself if this should is really *your* value or if it is a value you adopted without giving it specific thought. Is it being applied in too rigid a way in this situation?

Imagine it's your first semester at college, for instance, and your report card is marked with two As, three Bs, and one B-. Because you've always done fairly well in school, you immediately think that you should have made all As. You feel that you should be upholding higher academic standards. Otherwise you are a worthless student. It can help you to think, "Is this really how I feel about my performance? I know that I'm smart and that I work hard—am I being too unrealistic and hard on myself? Are these standards damaging my self-esteem?" If so, adjust your expectations to be more flexible and realistic given your situation.

Self-Blame

· · · · · · · ·

Self-blame is a self-esteem wrecker that has you blaming yourself for everything. It doesn't matter if you're at fault or not—you blame yourself for things that are only minimally under your control. This can include blaming yourself for your health, appearance, relationships, and so on. While it's good to take responsibility for your life, you take this to an extreme and see yourself as pathologically responsible.

An easy way to recognize this self-esteem wrecker is to notice whether you find yourself constantly apologizing. Your friend is late, but you apologize for being annoyed. Your boss asks you to make a few changes on your project, and you say, "I'm so sorry I did such a lousy job!" This is a habit that can blind you to your good qualities and accomplishments. If you're still close friends with all of your college roommates except for one who doesn't return your calls, you conclude that you must be unworthy of this person's friendship. However, the truth is, you are not always the cause for other people's actions.

Rebecca worked at a small community newspaper, where she wrote a weekly column. Her writing stimulated many readers to write letters to the editor. Sometimes they agreed with her point of view, other times they disagreed, but many of the disagreeing readers made a special point of mentioning that they respected her writing nonetheless. For the most part, her employers were satisfied with her work and enjoyed her presence in the workplace.

Although she seemed rather secure in her position, inside Rebecca couldn't fully accept her status as a valued writer as reality. Every time a reader disputed her fact checking or questioned her bias, she immediately blamed herself for not being thorough or sharp enough.

When her supervisor asked her about a detail in one of her articles, she would apologize and feel guilty before she even knew if she was wrong.

This became uncomfortable for her co-workers. They didn't want to ask Rebecca a question that would only instigate an apology. Her incessant habit of self-blame became a hindrance—others withheld helpful comments because they anticipated her inability to take constructive criticism. She even ended up missing opportunities because of this self-negating habit.

Rebecca can easily learn to get a handle on this habit. Her instinct to apologize for everything is her immediate clue. She can learn to strike a balance between feeling responsible and feeling at fault. If you suspect yourself of falling into the habit of self-blame, force yourself to check it out. You do not need to demoralize yourself for having normal, human shortcomings. Everyone has areas where they can improve, but your shortcomings are not a reflection of some innate fault that you have.

Self-blame occurs when you kick yourself for things that aren't your fault. You blame yourself for being scatterbrained, not having a better job, not being a better parent, not being more supportive to your partner, and so on. You even blame yourself for things that are only marginally under your control, such as your bad health or how others react to you. A classic example of self-blame is when you've been down for a while and can't seem to "cheer up." You feel somehow disconnected and alone—and then you actually blame yourself for that: "It's my fault people can't stand to be around me right now."

Stop kicking yourself. Look for ways you have tried your best. Give yourself credit for the effort you make in life. Remember how your fears, hopes, abilities, knowledge, pain, and past conditioning affect you and your choices. You've had to cope with a lot.

Control Fallacy

. . . .

This self-esteem wrecker comes from a false sense of omnipotence. You feel yourself struggling to control every aspect of every situation. When something goes wrong, you're convinced you should have prevented it. You hold yourself responsible for a fight your child has at school, for your mother's pneumonia, for the outcome of a project shared by seven co-workers, and for the fact that you got a tax audit.

As a result, your self-esteem suffers from an overinvestment in the actions of others. You should suspect your pathological critic of using this fallacy when you think things like "I've got to make them understand" or "I'll make sure she says yes."

Lucinda and Will moved in together when they were in college. While they were in school, living the student lifestyle, they were compatible. Waking up, strolling to the coffee shop, eventually getting to the library by late afternoon—this pace worked for both of them. However, soon after graduation, Lucinda was ready for more.

She wanted to plan for the future and delve into a fulfilling career. She thought about one day having kids, a house, and a car that she didn't have to kick in the mornings to get it started. All of these feelings seemed natural. But when she looked at Will, she felt increasingly distressed. Will was still waking up and strolling to the coffee shop, meandering past the job bulletin on his way home, eventually arriving at his job in the bike shop.

Before they knew it, two years had gone by since graduation. Lucinda was busy running a local nonprofit center for women. Will was still changing tires at the bike shop. Lucinda often asked Will what his plans were, and he would promise that things would change soon. She felt resentment and a sense of failure every time she thought about Will's life. She thought to herself, "How can he be so goddamn happy? He isn't doing anything! Doesn't he care that we always have to take my car, since we can't go anywhere together on his bike?"

Lucinda and Will began having regular fights about Will's life. Lucinda felt it was her responsibility to jar Will out of his passivity. But no matter how many schedules and goals she helped him write for himself, Will spent his days at the bike shop. And Lucinda took on Will's failure as her own.

In this case, Lucinda is making herself miserable by trying to control Will's direction in life. She will never successfully change his course—only he has the power to make that choice. Lucinda can move out or try to enjoy Will as he is—but she can't make him someone else. Like Lucinda, you may have hurt your self-esteem by attempting to assume responsibility for things over which you have no control. It's usually disappointing and always painful.

With *control fallacies*, you tend to kick yourself for things that really aren't your responsibility. To combat this self-esteem wrecker, you must rigorously weed out judgmental statements and replace them with balanced ones. State the facts of the situation without attacking yourself, and use coping statements like "I'm one person. I can't control everything."

Imagine, for example, that you arrive at your elderly mother's house, only to find her in a state of panic because she hasn't finished packing and the airporter van is supposed to arrive at any minute. Your first instinct is to feel guilty and think, "It's all my fault! I should have been here to help pack!" Wait! It's not your fault. Stop bad-mouthing yourself. You're not responsible for your mother's life. You can start helping her now that you're at her house, but it's no use beating yourself up for something that isn't your responsibility.

Comparing

· · · · · · · ·

In a universe in which you compare yourself with others, every action, statement, or event seems to have something to do with you. You take the world personally. You enter a crowded room and begin wondering who is smarter, better looking, more competent, and so on. This puts an awful lot of pressure on your self-esteem, because instead of having a consistent sense of self, the way you feel about yourself depends on how you measure up to everything around you. You may think you're looking pretty good until your friend comes over and you think he or she looks better. Now you think you look bad, simply because you're seeing yourself only by contrast.

Frank, for example, always viewed himself as a smart guy. As a child, he was a compulsive reader, immersing himself in whatever books his family had in the house. He would read everything from Greek mythology and the literary classics to scientific literature and theory. He was just interested and curious about knowledge in general. In college he started off as a premed major, but he ended up with a degree in English literature. While he was in school, he met his future fiancée, Emily, and they began living together.

Frank was a manager of a popular restaurant in the town where he and his girlfriend lived. He made good money there, so he kept his job after graduation. However, Emily, who had also been an English literature major, got a job on the local newspaper reviewing books. At first he thought he was happy for his girlfriend, but he began realizing that he felt oddly uncomfortable when she'd tell him about her job. He tried to be supportive and encouraging, but really whenever she talked about a book she needed to find to review, or a compliment she had received on a recent review, Frank felt his self-esteem shrinking.

Hearing about Emily's accomplishments became a siren to his ears. For Frank, her success began to simply mirror his lack of intellectual expression. When Frank read the paper and saw her name, all he could think of was himself working at the restaurant. Next to hers, his life felt like a waste. Because he could only see himself in contrast with or in relation to her life, he began to feel he was living under tremendous pressure. The pressure wasn't even definable; he just knew he was lacking.

He began fighting, striking out verbally whenever Emily tried to talk about her work. It got so bad that he began to act as if he didn't want to hear about anything intellectual in an attempt to prove to himself that he didn't care anyway. Frank's behavior was offensive and painful for Emily. She knew he was an intelligent and interesting person, so his resentment confused her.

It's difficult to catch yourself indulging in the comparing self-esteem wrecker. One way is to pay close attention when someone is telling you a story about his or her own experiences. Do you instantly judge your own performance according to their account? Do you suddenly see yourself as lesser than or better than? Do you see yourself as flawed by comparison? Do you usually feel bad when comparing?

If you constantly compare yourself with others in terms of abilities, traits, and achievements, you need to take a look at your balancing strengths. Find things you can celebrate about yourself. Instead of thinking, "She's smarter and better looking than me," say to yourself, "Hey, I'm good at listening and problem solving, and I'm a totally committed friend." You need to concentrate on affirming your own right to be exactly as you are, without apology or judgment. If you're going to the movies with a friend who's full of sophisticated commentary, you may be tempted to see yourself as someone who knows nothing at all about film. Stop it! Focus on something you're proud of and skip torturing yourself with worthless who's-doing-it-better comparisons.

PART IV

Revision Your Development

The revisioning technique comes out of the work of John Bradshaw and other therapists and writers who have studied the roots of people's feelings of shame and unworthiness, addictive cravings, and codependency. The basic idea is that within yourself you have many selves of all different ages—an inner infant, an inner toddler, an inner adolescent, and so on. These selves are "frozen" at various, younger stages of development, unaware of the experiences and skills you gained at a later age. Using a visualization technique, you can comfort, heal, and teach these earlier versions of yourself. This reduces the pain and negative effect of hurtful early memories.

Revisioning Your Infancy

· · · · · · · · · · · · · · · · · ·

Using visualization, you can contact your inner child at the youngest age and imagine receiving perfect, loving care from your adult self. It's like remaking the movie of your life, rewriting sad scenes and giving the movie a happy ending.

Your unconscious mind doesn't believe in time. To your unconscious mind, things that happened when you were six months old can be just as important and immediate as things that happened yesterday. This means that deep inside, your entire infant personality survives intact in every detail, with no knowledge of any older versions of you. You are now going to visit this strange and special version of yourself. To get the most out of this exercise, record the instructions and play them back so you don't have to remember all the steps and wording.

Lie down, close your eyes, and relax. Scan your body from head to toe, relaxing any muscles that seem tense. Pay attention to your breathing and allow it to get slow and deep.

When you are calm and relaxed, imagine that you are standing outside the home you lived in when you were born. Study the building's size, shape, color, and texture. Notice any landscaping you remember or the cars of the day going down the street. Feel the sun on your skin, the coolness of the breeze, the sounds of birds or dogs or traffic.

Go into the home and find the room where you slept when you were born. If you don't know or don't remember what it looked like, imagine the earliest bedroom you can recall. In the room is a crib. In the crib is a baby sleeping. The baby is you.

Study your tiny fingers with their perfect nails, your little mouth, your wispy baby hair. What kind of diaper or sleeper does the baby have on? What color is the baby blanket? The more details you add, the more real this moment will become for you.

Now imagine that your infant child wakes up and starts crying. Really hear the wails of protest getting louder and louder. Now see your mother, father, or whoever took care of you coming in the room. They can't see the adult you. You're invisible. Watch your parent or other caretaker coping poorly with your infant needs—being impatient and angry, handling you roughly or carelessly, failing to cuddle or talk to you, failing to realize that you need to be changed or fed. See and hear your infant self continue to fuss.

Now remake the scene. Wind the film back to where the baby wakes. This time, you go to the crying baby and pick it up. Cuddle and hug your infant self. Give the baby some milk from a bottle. Talk to your infant self as the crying stops and the baby smiles up at you in angelic wonder and contentment. Say to your infant self phrases such as:

- Welcome to the world.

- There's never been anyone else exactly like you before.

- I love you just the way you are.

- I'll never leave you.

- I'm going to take care of everything you need.

- You're just acting normally for your age.

- You have no real choices to make right now.

Hug your infant self one more time and put the baby down. Say good-bye and promise to return soon. Turn and leave the room.

Now rewind the film again and imagine being your infant self, held, fed, and loved by the perfect parent, your future self. Try to get a sense of how vulnerable and helpless you were.

When you are ready to end the visualization, remind yourself of your surroundings and open your eyes. Use this visualization whenever you feel overwhelmed or insecure.

Revisioning Your Toddler Years

· · · · · · · · · · · · · · · · · · · ·

While you were very young, parental messages shaped your basic sense of worth. In this visualization you will imagine yourself as a toddler and give yourself empowering messages of autonomy and worth. It's a chance to counteract early experiences of being shamed and put down.

To your unconscious mind, things that happened to you at age two or three are just as fresh and relevant as this morning's news. There is a two-year-old and a three-year-old version of you, deep inside, that still feels the hurts and fears that cut so deeply at that age. You can go back now and relieve some of those barely remembered feelings.

To get the most out of this visualization, record the instructions so you don't have to memorize everything. Lie down, close your eyes, and relax. Scan your body, starting at your head and working slowly down to your feet, searching for any tense muscles and willing them to relax. Breathe slowly and deeply, relaxing more and more profoundly.

When you are deeply relaxed, imagine that you are standing outside the home you lived in when you were a toddler. See the colors and shapes of the building before you. Pay attention to the weather, the sounds, and other surroundings.

Go into the home and look around. Notice any furniture or special toys you remember. If details are unclear, make some up that seem plausible. Now you are going to visualize one of the earliest scenes you can remember. Pick a time when you were unhappy, when something bad happened that hurt. It can be a real memory or it can be based on a story your family told you later. Don't worry if you get some details wrong. The exercise will work anyway.

See yourself in the situation. How are you dressed? What color is your hair? How long is it? Are you starting to resemble one of your parents or siblings? Watch the painful scene begin—when you broke something, when someone abandoned you, when you were spanked or scolded. See how upset your inner child becomes. Concentrate on the details: the sights, sounds, smells, tastes, and feelings.

When the scene is over, take your toddler self aside, into another room or some other safe place. Tell your toddler self:

- I am you, from the future when you're all grown up.

- I love you.

- There's never been another kid like you.

- I like you just the way you are.

- I'll never leave you.

- You're acting normally for a child your age.

- It's not your fault. You have no choice in the matter.

- You're doing the best you can to survive this hard time.

- It's perfectly all right to explore.

- I'll protect you while you learn about the world.

- I love taking care of you.

- You have a right to say no.

- It's okay to be angry, scared, or sad.

- I love watching you grow up and become your own person.

Hug your toddler self, say good-bye, and promise to return soon. Turn and leave the room.

You should "rewind" and repeat this visualization twice. The first time you repeat the exercise, imagine it from the point of view of the toddler. The second time, imagine that you are the toddler again but you already know that you will survive, that it will turn out all right. In this last version, see yourself acting calmer and braver in the scary situation.

When you are ready to end the visualization, remind yourself of your surroundings and open your eyes. You should repeat this visualization for any painful memories you retain from ages two to three, or use it when you feel abandoned, put down, or ashamed.

Revisioning Your Preschool Inner Child

• • • • • • • •

In this visualization you get a chance to remake the movie of yourself from ages four to six. You can literally reprogram some of your earliest core beliefs about your abilities and competence.

Remember, deep within you, your unconscious mind holds a version of yourself that knows nothing past kindergarten. You can access that earlier self and correct self-concepts you formed with the magical but uniformed mind of the preschool child. To get the most out of this visualization, record the instructions and play it back to yourself so you can concentrate on relaxing and remembering.

Lie down, close your eyes, and relax. Let your mind's eye go over your body from head to foot, sensing and relaxing tense muscles. Breathe more and more slowly, more and more deeply.

When you're well relaxed, imagine that you are standing in front of the home where you lived when you were four or five or six, before you entered the first grade. Notice the kind of house or apartment; observe the setting. Is it in the city or the country? Large or small? Quiet or noisy? Neat or messy?

Go into the home and find yourself at preschool age. Notice what you are wearing. How tall are you? Skinny or plump? Are there any favorite toys around? What color are your eyes? Are you dusty from playing outside or clean and rosy from a bath? Make up as complete a picture of your young self as you can.

Play out an unpleasant scene you remember from this time. It could be the fight with a family member, the scary time your parent came home drunk, the time your mom or dad just lost it and got hysterical, the time you got lost at the county fair, the time that the bully at day care threatened or attacked you. Notice how scared and/or confused your preschool self is. Observe how your inner child tries to understand and make sense of things, in spite of hurts and fears. Notice that your younger self lacks skills and knowledge that you now have.

When it's all over, take your inner child to a safe place and sit down together. Tell your younger self that you are from the future, that you can be the good parent who is missing, and that your preschool self can count on you. Put your arm around your younger self and say:

- I love you.
- I'm glad you're a girl (or boy).
- You're the only one like you in the world, and I like you the way you are.
- You're doing your very best right now.
- You just don't have much power to change what's going on right now.
- You're acting normally for a kid your age.
- I'll help you figure out how to protect yourself.
- It's okay to cry.
- You're good at thinking for yourself.
- You're good at imagining things.
- I'll help you separate what's real from what's imaginary.
- You can ask for what you want.
- You are not to blame for your mom's and dad's problems.
- It's okay to ask me any questions.

Try to get a sense of how your inner child is interpreting the event. What does the child believe is happening? What does it mean to the child about his or her worth, safety, and belonging? Offer an explanation to your inner child that leaves her or him innocent and blameless for what happened.

You should "rewind" and repeat this visualization twice. The first time, imagine it from the point of view of your inner child, really feeling the pain and confusion, and then being calmed and comforted by your future self. The second time, imagine that you are the child again, but that this time you already know that you will survive, you will understand, and things will turn out all right. In this last version, see yourself acting calmer in the problem situation and "bouncing back" quickly.

When you are ready to end the visualization, remind yourself of your surroundings and open your eyes. You can repeat this visualization for any painful memories you retain from this time of your life, or use it whenever you feel dependent, ashamed, or guilty.

Revisioning Your
School-Age Inner Child

· · · · · · · · · · · · · · · ·

In this visualization you get to fix some things that went wrong in grammar school. Even though you may have a clear memory of being left out of every foursquare game from grades one through five, your unconscious mind can be fooled into thinking it happened differently. That's because your unconscious mind is no great fan of reality. Things that really happened and things that happen only in fantasy are all the same to your unconscious.

It's a good idea to record the instructions below and play them back as you recline with your eyes closed. Lie down, close your eyes, and relax. Systematically scan your body from feet to head for tension, and consciously relax any tight muscles you notice. Breathe slowly and deeply, willing your respiration and heart rate to slow.

When you feel relaxed, imagine that you're at your grammar school. Visualize the playground, cafeteria, classroom, or wherever you remember having a horrible experience that still makes you cringe to this day. Notice all the details of the kids, the teachers, the desks, the blackboards, and especially the smells of school: chalk, paste, bag lunches, crayons, pencil shavings.

Imagine the painful scene when you were humiliated in front of the whole class, when your so-called best friend betrayed you, when you were passed over or bullied, when you were made to feel stupid or clumsy or inadequate.

At the end of the scene, take your younger self aside and comfort the child. Put your arm around your inner child and say:

- I'm from the future; I'm you all grown up.

- I'll stand up for you.

- It's fine to try out new ideas and ways of doing things.

- You can make your own decisions.

- It's okay to disagree.

- You can trust your feelings.

- It's okay to be afraid.

- You can choose your own friends.

- How you dress is your business.

- You're acting normally for your age.

- You have no real choice in this matter; there's nothing else you could do.

- You are doing the best you can to survive.

Then say good-bye to your inner child, promising to return whenever you're needed. "Rewind" and repeat this visualization twice. The first time, imagine it from the point of view of your inner child, really feeling the doubt and frustration, and then being comforted by the meeting of your future self. The second time, imagine that you are the child again, but that this time you already know that you will survive, you will become an adult, and life will get better. In this last version, see yourself acting more confidently and competently in the problem situation, shrugging off the pain as a passing stage of grammar school melodrama.

When you are ready to end the visualization, remind yourself of your surroundings and open your eyes. You can repeat this for any painful memories. You can also use it whenever you feel discouraged about your competence or passed over by peers or authority figures.

Revisioning Your Inner Adolescent

· · · · · · · · · ·

Even people with high self-esteem can think of many painful memories dating from ages eleven through sixteen. In this visualization you will relive some of those memories, bringing to them adult perspectives and skills that you didn't possess and desperately could have used at the time.

As far as your mind is concerned, part of you is still an adolescent inside. All of your gawky teenage enthusiasms, hang-ups, and frustrations survive as an inner adolescent. Using your imagination, you can give your adolescent self a second chance at that first date, a way to avoid that first auto accident, or a way to negotiate on a more equal footing with parents and teachers.

You might want to record the instructions so that you can play them back as you concentrate on relaxation and intensifying your visualization. Lie down, close your eyes, and relax. Notice every major muscle group in your body from head to toe, willing your tight muscle fibers to let go and relax. Shift your attention to your breathing and let it slow down.

When you are completely relaxed, imagine a scene from your teenage years when you were suffering from low self-esteem. You might visualize a scene involving sex, conflicts at school, or rebellion against your parents. Pay attention to the sights and sounds, the people involved, and how you acted and reacted as an adolescent. Really get into the scene and remember as much detail as you can.

Watch the scene through to the end, then take your adolescent self to a safe place where you can share what you now know as an adult:

- I am from your future; I am you grown up.

- I'm here to tell you that you can find the right person to love.

- You can find something meaningful to do in life.

- It's okay to disagree with your parents.

- You are becoming an independent person.

- You can safely experiment with sex.

- It's okay to feel confused and lonely.

- You have lots of new and exciting ideas about life.

- It's okay to be wrapped up in yourself now.

- It's normal to be ambivalent.

- It's all right to feel embarrassed and awkward.

- No matter how far out you go, I'll be there for you.

- You're acting normally for your age.

- You're doing the best you can to survive.

Look for a positive way to interpret your adolescent self's behavior. Hug and reassure your younger self. Say good-bye and promise to return whenever you're needed. Then rerun this scene from your adolescent point of view, and enjoy being comforted and supported by your older self. Finally, run through the scene once more, acting as you might have been able to if you had had all your current adult knowledge, experience, and skills.

When you're ready, remind yourself of your surroundings and open your eyes. You can repeat this visualization for any painful memories from your adolescence, or use it whenever you feel rebellious, confused, or misunderstood.

Revisioning Your
Young Adulthood

. . . .

You may still consider yourself a young adult, or your young adulthood may be many decades in the past. No matter how long ago it was, you can undoubtedly remember certain painful episodes when you felt ashamed, incompetent, or stupid trying to adapt to adult life. This visualization applies the inner child visualization technique to these more recent memories.

Remember that your unconscious mind exists outside of time and the normal constraints of linear reality. You can use your imagination to change the past and alter the reality your unconscious mind remembers. Have you ever come away from an embarrassing incident rehearsing the witty remarks and slick moves that you wish you had made? Well, this exercise gives you the chance to travel back in time and make the "coulda, shoulda, woulda's" come true.

Consider taping the following instructions so that you don't have to remember them during the visualization. Lie down, close your eyes, and relax. Scan your major muscle groups for tenseness, releasing tight muscles systematically from head to toe. Inhale and exhale slowly and deeply, paying attention to the air sighing softly in and out of your lungs.

When you are sufficiently relaxed, imagine a scene from your young adult life when you broke up with someone, lost a job, failed in school, made a bad decision, damaged a friendship, or experienced some other painful event. Set the scene for yourself with all the people, places, and things necessary to make the memory come to life. Use your senses of sound, sight, smell, taste, and touch. Watch the scene and notice what you said and did to contribute to the unfortunate outcome.

When the scene is over, take your younger self aside and introduce yourself as a more grown-up version from the future. Comfort your young adult self by saying:

- You will learn how to love and be loved.

- I know you will make a difference in the world.

- You can be a success on your own terms.

- You're acting normally for your age.

- You're doing the best you can to survive.

- Often you have no choice in the matter.

Include a positive interpretation of your younger self's behavior. Give your younger self a hug and say good-bye. Promise to return whenever you are needed.

Rerun this scene from your young adult's point of view, and enjoy being reassured and supported by your older self. Then run through the scene once more, acting as you might have if you had it to do over again today, with a more mature perspective. Congratulate yourself on what you have survived and learned in life.

When you're ready, remind yourself of your surroundings and open your eyes. You can repeat this visualization for any painful memories from your adult life that make you feel discouraged—about work, money, or love.

PART V

Find Compassion

Compassion literally means "to feel with." To learn compassion, you first learn to feel with others. You practice understanding their emotions, their motivations, their fears, and their hopes. Above all, you come to the stunning realization that everyone, even the apparent villains, is doing what appears best at the time.

Once you can sense some compassion for others, you start on yourself. This is more difficult. It's easier to ignore or forgive failings in others than in yourself. But gradually you will understand why you do what you do, why you feel what you feel. Finally, you will come to the liberating notion of your own good intentions—that even you are doing your best, according to your fullest understanding of the current situation.

Compassion for Someone Who's Hurt You

$\bullet \quad \bullet \quad \bullet \quad \bullet \quad \bullet \quad \bullet \quad \bullet \quad \bullet \quad \bullet \quad \bullet$

As a kid, you may have played the game where you show off all of your scars to the other kids. Remember? It was always fun and dramatic, because it gave you a chance to tell the great story of how you got each wound, and it let you hear other kids' stories.

The stories behind emotional scars aren't usually so fun to recall. If you've been emotionally hurt (as all of us have), you will most likely have a few scars to show for it. Like physical scars, these will be noticeable but faded, because they are essentially healed.

Unfortunately, a lot of folks have emotional *wounds* rather than scars. The damage they've suffered hasn't ever healed, and so the wound remains open and painful. If someone has hurt you in the past, compassion can be a powerful balm to aid in healing. Understanding, accepting, and forgiving that person will give your wound a chance to mend and can give you relief from the pain this wound continues to cause you.

The following visualization gives you a chance to let go of your anger and pain from a past wound by opening your heart to the person who hurt you. It's useful to make a tape recording of the instructions to play as you visualize. As you record, remember to speak slowly, in a low, distinct, relaxed tone.

Lie on your back with your hands and arms uncrossed and your legs stretched out. Close your eyes and take several deep breaths. Continue to breathe deeply and slowly as you scan your body for tension. As you notice tight areas, relax your muscles and settle into a heavy, warm, relaxed state. Let your breathing slow even further, and suspend your judgments. Accept whatever images come into your mind, even if they don't immediately make sense.

Imagine that there is a chair in front of you. Someone is sitting in the chair, someone who has hurt you in some way. Imagine that person who has hurt you sitting silently in the chair. Notice the details of the person's appearance: how big they are, what color their clothes are and how they fit, the person's posture. The person is looking calmly and expectantly at you. Say to the person:

You are a human being, like me. When you hurt me, you were just trying to survive. You did your best, given your limitations and your understanding of the situation at the time. I can understand your motivations, your fears, and your hopes. I share them because I am human too. I may not like what you did, but I understand it.

I accept the fact that you hurt me. I don't like it, but I don't condemn you for doing it. Nothing can change what happened. I forgive you. I may not approve or agree, but I can forgive. I can let go of the past and wipe the slate clean. I know I can't expect atonement. I am letting go of revenge and resentment. Our differences are in the past. I'm in control of the present, and I can forgive you now. I can leave my anger behind.

Continue looking at the person and gradually open your heart. Open yourself, letting the anger and resentment fade out like music being turned down. If it's difficult to empathize or let go of your anger, don't judge yourself. Go at your own pace and be easy on yourself. When you are ready, say "I forgive you" one more time. Let the image of the person in the chair fade slowly from sight.

This visualization is particularly helpful right after someone has mistreated you or when something from your past keeps getting in the way of your focusing clearly on the present.

Compassion for Someone You've Hurt

• • • • • • • •

On the long road of life, everyone collects a certain amount of baggage. Even if you do your best to travel light, you often find yourself toting a big sack of memory that slows you down and makes your journey a lot more arduous. For many folks, the biggest, heaviest, and most cumbersome piece of baggage they haul down the road is guilt. The frustrating thing about guilt is that it doesn't do you much good, but it sure can slow you down. Wouldn't it be great to unload some of that baggage?

The following visualization provides you with an opportunity to unpack a little. If you've hurt someone in the past and carry around a lot of guilt about it, here's a chance to begin lightening your load.

As with any visualization, it's a good idea to make a tape recording of the instructions to play while you visualize. Remember to record using a slow, soft, relaxed, yet distinct tone.

Sit or lie down, close your eyes, and begin to relax. Take several deep, slow breaths. Keep breathing deeply and slowly as you scan your body for tension. If you find a tight area, relax the muscles until your entire body feels heavy, warm, and still. Let your breathing slow down even more as you let go of judgments. Let images come to mind without judging them, even if they don't seem to make sense at first.

With your eyes closed and your breathing slow, visualize a chair in front of you. There is someone sitting in the chair—someone you've hurt, someone from whom you want understanding, acceptance, and forgiveness. Imagine all the details of the person: what they're wearing, how they're sitting, the way their hands are placed. See them as clearly as you can. The person looks at you calmly and expectantly as you say:

I am a human being, just like you. We are both simply trying to survive. When I hurt you, I was trying to do what seemed best for me at the time. If I had then the awareness I have now, I would have chosen differently. But at the time I could only do what I did. I understand that I hurt you, and I want you to know that hurting you was not my goal.

Please accept the fact that I hurt you and nothing can change that. I would undo it if I could—but I can't. Nothing now can change the past. Please forgive me. I don't ask that you approve of what I did or agree with me, only that you forgive me. I want to put our differences in the past, wipe the slate clean, and start over. Please open your heart to me—understand, accept, and forgive.

As you look at the person you hurt, see them slowly smile. Know that you are understood, that you are accepted, and that you're forgiven. Let the image of the person fade away slowly until the chair is empty.

Compassion for Yourself

· · · · · · · · · · · · · · · · ·

Everyone loves Wendy. She's the kind of person who seems to have a never-ending supply of love and generosity to offer. She's always the first to embrace someone new and the last to pass judgment. Wendy is the woman who spends her whole vacation helping take care of her sick neighbor—the same neighbor who rear-ended her the year before, totaling both cars. It seems as if Wendy can let go of any negative feeling—she never participates in blaming and is always willing to forgive.

That's why it's so confusing to everyone to see how she's acting in response to her son's expulsion from school. She's upset with her son, of course, but what's surprising is that she just can't seem to be able to forgive *herself* for her son's problems. She's gone on long, guilty rants about her failures as a parent to several of her close co-workers, and her obvious depression is starting to affect her work. How is it that Wendy can forgive everyone except herself?

One of the most challenging aspects of improving your compassion skills is feeling true compassion for yourself. Yet compassion for yourself is essential, not only to make you feel better about yourself, but also to allow you to continue to feel compassion for others. The amount of compassion in the world is not limited—on the contrary, it replenishes and increases each time it's expressed. That's why compassion for yourself isn't ever an indulgence but always a *necessity*.

Use the following visualization to help you extend compassion to yourself. Make a tape recording of the directions to listen to during your visualization. When you speak into the recorder, use a low, soft, relaxed, but distinct tone.

Sit or lie down and close your eyes. Relax your body while taking deep, slow breaths. Scan your body for any tension, and relax any tight areas while continuing to breathe slowly and deeply. Continue until your body feels warm, heavy, and still.

Imagine a chair in front of you. See yourself sitting in the chair. Notice all the details of your appearance: how you're dressed, your posture, the way your hands and legs are positioned. Hear yourself saying:

I am a human being. I'm worthwhile simply because I exist and try to survive. I take care of myself. I take myself seriously. I correctly take myself into consideration in all matters. I have legitimate needs and wants. I can choose what I need and want without having to justify it to anybody. I make choices, and I take responsibility for them. I always do my best. Each thought and action is the best I'm capable of at the time.

Because I'm human, I make mistakes. I accept my mistakes without blame or judgment. When I make a mistake, I try to learn from it. I am imperfect, and I forgive myself for my mistakes. I know that others are equally worthy, equally imperfect. I have compassion for them because they are engaged in the same struggle for survival that I am.

Visualize the imaginary you getting out of the chair, coming over to where the real you is, and sitting or lying down in your body, merging into one person. Relax and rest. You are at peace with yourself and at peace with others.

Compassion for Things Past

· · · · · · · · · · · · · · · · ·

Colette had no trouble feeling compassion for others, and she could even work up a mild feeling of warmth toward her present-day self. But she could never forgive herself for crippling her ex-boyfriend Randy. He'd shown up drunk one night, begging her loudly to "Give me a second chance." She'd yelled "Get out, get out, get out . . ." until he left, burning rubber in reverse, making black skid marks that would take three years to fade. Ten minutes later he had run a stop sign and hit a truck. Colette still felt guilty every time she saw Randy limping around town.

Are you good at feeling compassion for others while simultaneously beating yourself up about past events? Experiencing true compassion means forgiving and understanding others—and sometimes telling that critic inside your head to go jump in the lake. If your inner critic insists on hassling you about something that happened in the past, the following exercise can help.

Select an event from the past that your pathological critic has used to attack you. It can be anything you've labeled as bad: not visiting your parent enough, your eating binge last week, the argument with your friend or co-worker.

Now get into a comfortable position and close your eyes. Take a few deep breaths and scan your body for any tension, stretching and relaxing any tight areas. Begin to drift backward in time, back to the event you've chosen. Imagine the time and the event in detail—see what you were wearing, hear any conversation going on in the room, and notice any feelings you were having at the time of the event, either physical or emotional.

Now, while holding onto the image of yourself in the middle of the event, ask yourself this question: "What need was I trying to meet?" Think about it. Were you trying to feel more secure, more in control, and/or less anxious? Was there some sort of pain you were trying to avoid?

Now ask: "What was I thinking at the time?" What were your beliefs about the situation? How were you interpreting things?

Finally, ask yourself: "What kind of pain or feeling was influencing me?" Review the entire emotional context of the event.

When you've taken plenty of time to get some answers to these questions, the next step is to accept and forgive yourself for who you were at that moment in time. Stay focused on the image of yourself in the midst of the past event, and say to the person you were: "I wish this hadn't happened, but I was trying to meet my needs. I accept myself without judgment for my attempt. I accept myself at that moment as trying to survive the best way I could." Really try to feel each of these statements, allowing them to really sink into your consciousness.

Now it's time to let go of the past. Say to yourself: "I owe no debt for this mistake. It's over and I can forgive myself."

Keep using this exercise for as many past events as you can. As you use it, compassion for yourself will come more easily and automatically, and you'll feel less caught in painful regrets of the past.

Compassionate Listening

· · · · · · · · · · · · · ·

Everybody loves Mabel because she's so understanding. She sympathizes when her car's not ready and the mechanic complains about the jerks at the parts counter. She's the only one who knows why her nephew would rather be Spiderman than Batman. She's the one Aunt Rose comes to when Uncle Roger's Alzheimer's gets to her. The secret of Mabel's compassionate understanding is not a Ph.D. in psychology—it's that she really listens when others are speaking.

The three-step exercise that follows will help you practice your active listening skills with a variety of people. As you listen with an ear to understanding, feel your sense of compassion for others—and for yourself—expand.

First, practice the following exercise with a friend. Tell your friend that you're trying to improve your listening skills, and ask him or her to tell you a story. The story should be about something important in your friend's life—a past trauma, a happy childhood memory, or a hope for the future.

As your friend talks, your job is to listen carefully and ask questions about any parts you don't understand. Ask your friend to clarify or expand, and encourage your friend to talk about his or her thoughts and feelings: "Why was that important to you?" "How did you feel about that?" "What did you learn from that?"

Occasionally paraphrase what you hear: "So, in other words, you . . ." This is important because it helps you remove your own false interpretations and clarify your friend's precise meaning. Let your friend correct your perception of the story, then incorporate these changes into the paraphrase. This way you'll know that you've actively listened, and your friend will feel heard.

Next, move to a more difficult step: practicing compassionate listening with acquaintances. Choose people that you don't know very well and practice your empathetic listening without their knowing.

Whatever they're talking to you about, ask for clarification and expansion. Resist jumping in with a story of your own. Notice when you start judging them and set the judgments aside. You don't have to love the person—just try to understand what they say without letting your judgments get in the way.

Paraphrasing is even more important with an acquaintance. You gain a deeper understanding of an unfamiliar story and the other person feels heard. As you actively listen, true opinions and feelings may emerge as the speaker learns that you're a careful, interested listener. Do this exercise often enough, and acquaintances can become friends.

The last step is practicing this exercise with strangers. At a party or get-together, choose someone you don't know or even someone you know but don't like. Engage them in conversation and use your active listening skills to really understand what the person has to say. Remember to listen carefully, suspend judgment, and paraphrase.

When you're listening to someone you actually don't like, it's important to remember the basic tenet of compassion: everyone is simply trying to survive, just like you are. Ask yourself the three questions that lead you into a compassionate response toward another person: What need is this person meeting by saying this? How is it making this person feel better? What beliefs are influencing them?

PART VI

Achieve an Accurate
Self-Assessment

I s your mind a room full of fun-house mirrors that magnify your flaws and hide your virtues? If you're lost in the not-so-fun house of low self-esteem, learning accurate self-assessment is the way out. It's difficult, but well within your reach, to change the habits of your lifetime—to remove the blinders, open your eyes, and turn away from the distortions of the fun-house mirrors that surround you.

The exercises in this section could be likened to writing your autobiography or painting a self-portrait. You will learn to avoid writing a critical exposé or painting a harsh caricature. You'll learn to tell your life's story objectively and paint your true features. You will affirm the good, acknowledge the bad, and realize that the truth comes in all colors, not just black and white.

Affirming the Good in You

· · · · · · · · · · · · · · ·

Ever since French pharmacist Emil Coué introduced the phrase "Every day in every way I am growing better and better," people have used affirmations. It's a way of weaving key truths and beliefs into your everyday life. Daily affirmations can strengthen your core sense of worth. Each time you affirm the good in yourself, you're pushing away the old negative messages from your past.

You took a lot of blows growing up—everyone does. The ways you were labeled then still affect you. Instead of your parents' voice, now it's your own inner monologue that whispers, "You're stupid," or "You're so lazy." It's called introjection—taking on the judgments of others as your own judgments of yourself. Affirmations can be a shield against that voice. You stop listening because there's something new and positive to hear instead.

Take a look at your list of strengths and positive qualities. Select one that you'll make into an affirmation today. It should be a positive, one-sentence statement, such as:

- I've always been loyal to my friends.

- I am good.

- I try hard with the important things I do.

- I'm a generous person.

- I have strong, hard-working hands.

- I have a curious, creative mind.

- I am good at making quiet, peaceful times.

- My face is attractive.

- I am a sweet person.

- I have made my body strong and healthy.

- I am good to my children (parents, friends, etc.).

- I try to do what's right.

- I'm the best short-order cook in three counties.

- I can do the Sunday *New York Times* crossword.

Write a new affirmation each morning. Make it something you're proud of, something that feels really true about yourself. Keep the affirmation in mind throughout the day by developing a reminder signal to trigger it. For example, you can shift your watch to the opposite wrist each day. Looking for your watch can then be a reminder to use the affirmation.

By making affirmations a part of your daily life, you can continue to reinforce your self-esteem.

Giving an Example

• • • • • • • • • •

Remember how history teachers made up sadistic test questions like "Give three examples of ways the Enlightenment affected political process?" Your heart would sink. But they were good questions, because you had to understand a concept well enough to recognize concrete examples. This same process of illuminating a concept with an example can play a crucial part in raising your self-esteem. For instance, affirming the general principle that you have a curious, creative mind can be helpful. But you won't fully integrate that belief until you've identified concrete times and situations when you've been curious and creative.

Finding examples of the good in yourself takes a little work. Not because it isn't there, but because—like in the case of the history test—it requires combing through the past for particular instances of a general principle.

Each day, starting today, choose a different item from your list of strengths and daily affirmations (from the previous exercise) for an exercise called *active integration*. Active integration transforms your strengths and positive qualities from a lot of words into specific memories. It helps you *believe* that these positive qualities really apply to you.

Try to think of at least three examples from your past of the strength or affirmation that you are highlighting that day. Write them down in a notebook or journal. Review the journal periodically to remind yourself of how your positive qualities get expressed in real life.

Here's the first three days of a pharmacist assistant's journal:

Positive Affirmation/ Strength	Examples
I'm good with my hands.	Made the form and poured the slab for my mother's patio.
	The realistic way I built my model railroad.
	Built the frame for Susan's foam bed (plus her planter boxes).
I'm good at making friends.	How easily I struck up a conversation with Keith at the concert.
	How I helped Nancy get insurance authorization for that old-fashioned drug her doctor prescribed, and we fell into the big conversation about our favorite authors.
	How Shariff and I got to talking about antioxidants at the counter.
I'm careful with people's feelings.	Didn't remind Jill about how she used to hate her father when she was reminiscing about her good times with him during his memorial service.
	Susan wore this totally ugly outfit, and I kept my mouth shut.
	Didn't say anything when Bill spilled the milkshake in my car—even though I was out of my mind.

Taking an Honest
Look at Yourself

· · · · · · · · · · ·

Adepressed neurosurgeon once confided to a colleague that, all things considered, he'd made rather a "botch" of his life. The colleague was flabbergasted. "You're senior staff at one of the most prestigious training hospitals in the country, and I suspect when you kick off they'll name a wing after you. I'm looking, but I can't find the botch."

The praise had zero impact. "This is a feeling," the doctor said. "This is how I feel about my life. The facts are irrelevant."

But the facts are *very* relevant, even though it doesn't seem that way when you're down on yourself. In this chapter you'll have an opportunity to take a detailed and honest look at yourself—your strengths and your weaknesses—to help you form a more accurate picture of the real you.

Draw a line down the middle of a piece of paper. Label the left-hand column "weaknesses" and the right-hand column "strengths." You can structure your exploration by looking at the following seven key areas of living:

1. Daily tasks of living

2. Job performance

3. Mental functioning

4. Personality

5. Physical appearance

6. Relating to others

7. Romantic/sexual life

Start by listing every weakness you can think of in these seven key areas on the left-hand column of your paper. This should be easy. Most people are astoundingly good at labeling their flaws.

Now use the seven key areas to build a list of positive traits and qualities on the right-hand column of your paper. Think about the things you're proud of, the times when you've had success or experienced praise. Think about abilities, things you've mastered, things you've overcome. Include prizes, awards, and good marks for achievement. If this list doesn't have at least forty items, keep working on it until it does.

Some people are afraid to list the positive because it feels like bragging. They expect somehow to be slapped down for the audacity of celebrating their strengths. Don't let old habits of modesty or the fear of ridicule stop you. This is an honest inventory of strengths and weaknesses. It's neither fair to yourself nor helpful in this process to diligently list your flaws while failing to thoroughly investigate your strengths and positive qualities.

Once you've finished these two lists, you can go on to the next exercises in this section, which all require the completed lists.

Getting Rid of the Kickers

• • • • • • • • • • • • • • • • • • •

When people judge themselves, they often use negative labels like *stupid, fat, childish, crazy*—you name it. These terms have enormous power, and each time you use them they injure your self-esteem. A female security guard put it this way: "I go on these runs of self-hate. It feels like I'm a mule kicking myself. I keep saying, 'You're dumb. You're screwed up. You're a joke.'"

It's time to get rid of your own kickers. Go back to your list of weaknesses (from the previous exercise, "Taking an Honest Look at Yourself"). Taking the kickers out can most easily be accomplished by underlining each attacking label on your list. Then change it to something that's true but lacks the harsh connotations of the old words. Consider the word "phony." Aside from taking a meat hook to your self-esteem, the word implies that you're totally inauthentic. There's no way that's true, so "phony" needs to be rewritten in more neutral terms. For example, "I sometimes say things that are more flattering or positive than my true feelings."

If you've written "chipmunk cheeks" when describing your physical appearance, change it to "large, round cheeks." "Scrawny" should be crossed out and rewritten as "very slender." "Know nothing" should be edited to read "little knowledge about current events." "Blabbermouth" should be rewritten as "take up more than my share of the conversation." "Lazy" should be changed to "can't motivate myself to study." "Totally neurotic" might be revised as "fearful of rejection." There's nothing wrong with honestly facing your weaknesses, but make a commitment to yourself right now to use language that doesn't kick.

This exercise is a vital first step in the "telling the truth" process that is continued in the next exercise.

Telling the Whole Truth

· · · · · · · · · · · · · · ·

Edit your weaknesses as if you were an objective expert witness, sworn to tell the truth, the whole truth, and nothing but the truth. Take care, because language lies. It's easy to turn words against yourself, to describe your faults in such a way that peas seem the size of planets and a minor mistake is blown up into a catastrophic event.

Using truthful language to describe weaknesses will help protect your self-esteem. Truthful language is accurate rather than exaggerated. A commitment to accuracy means that you replace a term such as "potbelly" with an exact waist measurement. Instead of describing yourself as "passive sexually," you use the more accurate description that you are "cautious about initiating without seeing prior signals of interest." Instead of describing yourself as "illogical," you might more accurately say you are "unreasonable when angry." Rather than "scattered," you may be someone who is "easily distracted by anything interesting."

Note that accurate language is typically less stinging and hurtful. The focus is specific instead of general. It is rare to hear a truthful description that uses words like *everything, always, never, nobody, everyone,* and so on. Being specific means that you identify the exact times and situations when a weakness occurs; the fault becomes more limited and particular. Rather than a "lousy housekeeper," you may be someone who "cleans once a week but never picks up." Rather than "totally unmotivated," you might specifically say, "I wrote two short stories and a novel outline last year, though I didn't achieve all of my writing goals." Instead of "lose everything," you might "occasionally lose keys or notebook."

Return to your list of weaknesses and rewrite each so that it uses language that's accurate and specific. If you have difficulty with any item, ask yourself these questions:

- When and where do I do this?
- How often do I do this?
- Under what circumstances do I do it?
- With whom do I do it?
- Can I use a number or unit of measure to describe it?

Looking for Exceptions

· · · · · · · · · · · · · ·

There is hardly any weakness that doesn't have exceptions—and many even have corresponding strengths. One self-hating father, who signed himself "Spoil-Sport," wrote to Dear Abby that he'd "never played with his kids." But later in the letter he acknowledged that he'd read to them, took them to concerts and lectures, and helped his daughter develop her interest in math. This man may have genuine regrets that he didn't know how to have fun, but there was a balancing reality. He brought interest and enrichment into his children's lives.

A computer game programmer heaped scorn on herself for designing "testosterone trash." She hated the war games she spent her workday constructing, but ignored some important exceptions. There was the multiplication skills game she'd designed for her nephew, the computer class she taught at a private high school, and the computer-designed logos and artwork she had developed for a political action group.

Looking for exceptions and corresponding strengths is a vital step to reframing weaknesses that drag on your self-esteem. For example, a woman who considered herself "unable to ask for what I want" changed her mind when she identified key exceptions. "While I can't stand up to my family, I'm reasonably assertive with co-workers, my friends Annie and Simone, and kids at the preschool where I work." A man on a local school board saw himself as "lousy at arguing and debating." But on examination there were balancing strengths that more than made up for it: "I lack a killer instinct during arguments. What I like, though, is that I don't have to be right all the time. I look for ways to compromise and find common ground."

Return again to your list of weaknesses and, for every item where it's appropriate, write exceptions and balancing strengths. Ask yourself these questions to facilitate the process:

- Where, with whom, and under what circumstances have I ever done the opposite of the listed weakness?

- On what occasion(s) did I ever rise above this fault?

- Is there some good that has come of this weakness?

- Is there some way I've compensated for the weakness that I can be proud of?

- Is there a strength I can be proud of that is embedded in this weakness?

- Is there a strength that I display *despite* my weakness?

Remembering Your Good Points

$\bullet \quad \bullet \quad \bullet \quad \bullet \quad \bullet \quad \bullet \quad \bullet \quad \bullet$

Have you ever felt like you were walking around with a sandwich board advertising your flaws? Have you feared that your weaknesses were so obvious and your defenses so transparent that only the psychologically deaf and blind could fail to recognize them? Everyone who struggles with low self-esteem feels a constant and painful awareness of personal weaknesses. Betty, a fact checker for a magazine, put it this way: "It's like all my problems are written in neon. They flash so brightly I can't ever forget them."

What if you put the same effort into remembering strengths that you devote to monitoring your failings? What if you made a commitment to remind yourself of what you do right, what you're good at, and what you like about yourself? A surprisingly simple technique for remembering your strengths is to make reminder signs. Buy some three by five file cards, on which you can write one or more of the items from your strengths list. You can put these reminder signs on your shaving or vanity mirror, on the inside of your front door, on your closet or refrigerator, near a light switch, or inside your briefcase or gym bag. You can also put reminder signs on the back of a business card to keep in your desk drawer, in your wallet, or on your dashboard.

When you find an item from your strengths list that you wish to emphasize and remember, write it out on a card in a full sentence that's clear and affirmative. A horse trainer wrote these six reminder signs that she taped in various locations:

- I give my daughter time and attention.

- I took care of my father when he was sick.

- I've trained two excellent race horses.

- I stand up to things that are unfair.

- I take time to enjoy the morning light.

- I'm a good listener to my friends.

Notice that reminder signs about your strengths don't have to be anything big or extraordinary. It's enough to write down simple things that you appreciate about yourself.

If you're concerned that some of your signs might be read by others, you can avoid embarrassment by abbreviating your reminder. For example, the strength "creative at work" could show up on a sign as C.A.W. People could wonder, but they'd never guess.

Change your reminder signs every week or two so that you can highlight new strengths and qualities you're proud of. A good signal that signs need to be replaced is when they seem to recede into the background. If you aren't reading them, they aren't working. Rotating or changing them will recapture your attention.

Finding the Truth
You Missed

· · · · · · · ·

Voltaire once said that "The history of human opinion is scarcely more than the history of human errors." There's a reason for this. Most of our opinions—particularly those about ourselves—are formed when we're young. We then spend the rest of our lives gathering evidence that supports these core beliefs and ignoring everything to the contrary.

This tendency is called *confirmatory bias*, and because of it our beliefs rarely change or grow. We pay attention only to what we expect to see, and live our lives wearing psychological blinders. Self-esteem is very much affected by confirmatory bias. Negative beliefs about yourself don't change because you focus on negative parts of your experience while ignoring the positive. You remember the failures, the mistakes, the awkward and painful moments; you forget the praise, the goals met, the good works, and the appreciation of those who love you.

It's time to uncover the truth you've missed about yourself. You can reverse the effects of confirmatory bias by actively looking for evidence *against* old negative beliefs about your worth.

Across the top of a piece of paper write a core negative opinion about yourself (e.g., I'm stupid, I'm unlovable, I'm boring, I'm incompetent). Now for each decade of your life (ages 0–10, 11–20, 21–30, etc.) list every memory, every experience, every bit of evidence you can come up with that *contradicts* the core belief. This is important, so put some time into it. Comb through your history. Think of people and times and places where good things happened to you. Keep going, listing anything you can think of for each decade. When you're finished, rewrite the core belief so it reflects the truth you missed about yourself.

Here are some items from a list compiled by Jackie, a pizza delivery driver whose core belief was "I'm boring."

Age 0–10   Aunt Jen hung on my every word.

Age 11–20   Mary Jo and I talked for hours on the phone. Bill was always asking me out for a drive.

Age 21–30   I made my friend laugh so hard she wet her pants.

Jackie rewrote her belief to reflect a truth she discovered about herself: "Family and friends I've known a long time find me entertaining. If I'm boring to strangers, it's because I hold back and keep quiet."

Finding the truth you've missed will remove the blindness of conformity bias from your eyes and allow you to see yourself and others more accurately and compassionately.

Providing Tit for Tat

· · · · · · · · · · · · · ·

Chris walked into the conference room where he was due to give a presentation to his department. He was nervous because his boss was going to be there, and Chris had recently made some social gaffes in front of her. "Keep it short, now," he said to himself. "You always talk too damned much and get yourself into trouble."

He made his way to the front of the room, saying hello to everyone while he set up his materials. As he drew a diagram on the board he thought, "What a stupid drawing. These people are going to think I'm an idiot to even try to draw something out like this." He turned and tossed off a joke about the diagram. Everyone chuckled, but Chris thought, "I'm as funny as a heart attack."

Chris went ahead and gave his presentation, which to everyone in the room seemed to go off without a hitch. To everyone, that is, except Chris, whose constant stream of negative self-talk made him feel like a failure.

Does this story sound familiar to you? Many people spend a good part of each day pulling themselves down with negative thoughts about their performance at work, their looks, their success as parents, and so on. And, because they are constantly repeating these negative ideas, they believe them more and more deeply all the time.

Fortunately, this process can be reversed: You can use self-talk to *counter* negative beliefs about yourself. You have the power to effectively rewrite the story you tell yourself about you. And, because your beliefs are made up of these stories, the more you practice combating negative thoughts with positive self-talk, the stronger you'll feel about your many positive qualities.

The following exercise will help you combat your negative self-talk. You should practice it regularly—make it a discipline and a habit. The more automatic it becomes, the stronger you will feel.

All day, listen carefully to your own thoughts. Whenever you catch yourself making a negative self-statement ("I'm no good at cooking," "I'm a weak parent," etc.), write it down. Listen attentively to what you say to yourself. It's helpful to write down as many of your negative self-statements as you can.

In the evening, take some time to look at the list you've made. Then, after each of the negative statements you recorded, write down something *positive* about yourself. It can be anything—it doesn't have to do specifically with the negative statement. So, for example, if you wrote down, "I'm bad at small talk," you could write, "I'm good at long conversations," or even "I'm good at playing the guitar." Give yourself credit for all of your good qualities and all of your skills. You could list anything from your nice smile, to your generosity to your skill at juggling.

After you've completed your list, study it and notice how, for every negative thing you could say about yourself, you could just as easily say something positive. Now it's time to practice: The day after you make your list of positive rebuttals, go ahead and pay extra attention to your self-talk again. This time, on each occasion you find yourself saying something negative about you, counter it with a positive statement. It can be one of the positive statements from your list or something new. The important thing is that you counter each negative thought with a positive.

Practice this exercise each day for the next week, until it becomes a habit. Revisit it anytime you find yourself forgetting to counter negative self-talk with positive affirmations.

PART VII

Reframe Mistakes

Mistakes are inevitable. Since you can't avoid them entirely, you need to learn how to handle them, as this greatly determines their effect on your self-esteem. If you handle mistakes poorly, they can become devastating failures, world-shattering calamities, and carefully hoarded evidence of your low worth.

This section will teach you how to regard and handle mistakes so that they become reassuring evidence of your normality. Mistakes are merely temporary setbacks—life's little lessons in the school of endurable knocks.

Three Steps to
Handling Mistakes

• • • • • • • • • •

Margie had just enough time to get the cake baked before the dinner party. She'd worked most of the afternoon on the cake—her first baking project entirely from scratch. She wanted to impress folks at the party, and she was sure the cake would do the trick.

Suddenly she realized that she'd forgotten to pick up her dog, Max, from the veterinarian. Well, all she had to do was pop the cake in the oven . . . whoops. She'd forgotten to preheat. Well, no matter—she'd preheat the oven while she was at the vet. She set the oven, got her purse, and jumped in the car.

Half an hour later she rushed in with Max and ran directly to the kitchen. If she put the cake in the oven *right away* she'd be a little late to the party, but that was okay. She grabbed the cake pans, whirled around to slide them into the oven—and realized with an impressive chocolaty splatter that she'd forgotten to open the oven door. The pans crashed to the floor in a metallic cacophony, chocolate batter slid down the oven's front, and Margie slid to the floor in tears. It looked like the only one who'd be enjoying this cake was Max, who bowled Margie over as he rushed to gobble down the spoils.

When you're having a day like Margie's, nothing seems to go right, and you can hardly help blaming yourself for your mistakes. The following exercise will give you three steps to take when you begin the downward slide into self-blame over your mistakes.

The first step is to realize that everyone makes mistakes. Even those you most admire—those who are highly accomplished. That's because mistakes are an unavoidable byproduct of trying anything new. Make a list of historical or public figures who have made significant mistakes. Include only those people whom you respect and appreciate. Now make a second list of people you personally know and admire, and list their mistakes.

Why is it that even good and admirable people make mistakes? It's because they didn't recognize their decision as a mistake at the time they made it. They didn't fully realize the consequences of their act. Like anyone else, they could not predict with perfect accuracy the effects of a current decision on future experience.

The second step of this exercise is to recognize the inevitability of your own mistakes. Make a list of your ten biggest mistakes. Try not to beat yourself up as you do this—just sort through your past and dig up the ten mistakes that have had the most impact on your life.

Now, take the first item on your list and try to go back in your mind to the moment the decision was made. Try hard to remember your thoughts and feelings right before the act. Did you know what would happen, or did you hope for some happier consequence? Now try to remember the need or needs that pushed you into the decision. Recall the strength of those needs and how they influenced you. And here is the most important question: if you were to return to that time, with the *same* needs, perceptions, and predictions of future outcomes, would you act differently?

Now repeat this process with each mistake on your list. It may be necessary to skip some of the questions for a particular mistake if your memory is too hazy to really answer them.

The third step is to forgive yourself. You deserve forgiveness for your mistakes, no matter how painful the consequences. Why? Because you made the only decision you could make, given your needs and awareness at the time. Because you have already paid for your mistakes. It's impossible to learn without mistakes, and because the learning process continues your entire life, you will never stop making some instructive mistakes.

The Limits of Awareness

· · · · · · · · · · · · · ·

Sometimes making a mistake can make you feel really dumb, especially when it's a mistake you've made before. You may wonder to yourself why you can't seem to learn—why do you need to repeat the same mistake all the time?

There are many reasons why people make and repeat mistakes, but being "dumb" isn't actually one of them. More often, people repeat their mistakes because they are not aware of the consequences that came about the last time they made the mistake. They don't realize that the decision they are about to make is actually a mistake, so they go ahead and make the same mistake again and again.

Your awareness of the probable consequences of your actions is limited by five important factors:

1. **Ignorance.** Often you have no real way of predicting consequences because you have *never* been faced with similar circumstances before. You're flying blind. If you've never used spray paint before, you have no way of knowing that holding the nozzle too close causes the paint to run. If you don't know how to fold egg whites for your first soufflé, it might not rise properly.

2. **Forgetting.** There is no way to remember every consequence of every act you have ever performed. Many events are lost to awareness because they weren't sufficiently painful or important. As a result, you frequently repeat mistakes because you simply can't remember how things turned out last time. If you can't remember how much the mosquitoes tormented you the last time you went camping, you might forget to bring bug repellent again this year.

3. **Denial.** People deny and disregard the consequences of previous mistakes for one of two reasons: desire and fear. Sometimes they just want to drink and drive or eat a third dessert. Other times they are so afraid of change or of doing things differently that they deny or minimize the negative consequences of their mistakes. Faced with the same choice again, they make the same mistake because the alternatives seem too threatening. For example, Howard goes on dates and bores women to death with long recitations of his achievements. He suspects he might be turning them off but denies the consequences of his bragging, which results in few repeat dates and no relationships. He clings to denial because he's afraid of real communication, unwilling to risk talking about his authentic feelings.

4. **No alternatives.** Many mistakes are repeated because people simply lack the skills, ability, or experience to generate new strategies and solutions. For example, Connie keeps failing at job interviews because she stares at the floor, makes brief, one-sentence answers, and never says clearly, "I want this job."

5. **Habits.** Some habits, ingrained for a lifetime, prevent you from evaluating or even noticing your choices. You don't think about the consequences because you don't know you're making a decision. A classic example is choosing a short-range benefit while ignoring a long-range disaster, like the law school student who regularly chose the short-term pleasure of going out with friends rather than studying for his exams.

All of these factors can prevent you from making use of your experience. This happens to everyone at some point or another.

Go back to the list of ten mistakes that you made for the previous exercise, "Three Steps to Handling Mistakes." Take some time to consider each one, and decide which awareness-limiting factor affected your decision making at the time you made the mistake. Then forgive yourself for each mistake.

Mistakes Visualization

• • • • • • • • • • • • •

It takes practice to learn any new skill, whether it's cooking, pitching, or even learning to see mistakes differently. The following visualization exercise will help you practice thinking of mistakes as merely functions of limited awareness. Because no one can see into the future, no one can always accurately predict which decisions will turn out to be winners and which will turn out to be mistakes.

You may want to tape-record this visualization. Remember to speak slowly and distinctly.

Sit down in a comfortable chair or lie down on your back. Uncross your arms and legs. Close your eyes and take several deep, slow breaths. Feel yourself becoming more relaxed with each breath. Scan your entire body—limbs, chest, neck, and so on—for signs of tension. When you notice a tense spot, inhale, and with your exhale let go of that tension.

Continue breathing slowly and deeply, sinking further into relaxation. Now begin forming a picture of yourself in your mind. See yourself as you were when you recently made a mistake. Imagine all the details—where you were, what your face looked like, the position of your body. Watch yourself in the situation and notice how ignorance, forgetfulness, denial, habit, or lack of alternatives kept you from seeing any negative consequences. See how you made the mistake honestly, given your awareness at the time.

Remind yourself that you did your best at that moment in time. Say the following affirmations to yourself. Just let them drift into your mind:

- I am a unique and valuable human being.

- I always do the best I can.

- I love myself, mistakes and all.

Repeat these affirmations three or four times, changing the wording to suit your needs.

Now visualize yourself moving through your daily routine. See what you will be doing the rest of today or tomorrow. See that you are unique, that you are valuable, that you are trying to live the best way you can. Notice that you always try to do what seems best at the moment you do it.

Finish with this affirmation: Today I like myself more than yesterday. Tomorrow I will like myself more than today.

When you finish, open your eyes and get up slowly. As you go about your day, repeat the affirmations whenever they come to mind.

The exercise will work even better if you make up your own short, simple, positive affirmations. Remember, negative affirmations (such as "I will not criticize myself," as opposed to "I accept myself") tend to backfire. Keep the words in your affirmations positive.

To help you compose your own self-esteem affirmations, here is a list of some that have worked well for others.

- I'm basically fine as I am.

- It's okay to meet my needs as I see fit.

- I do the best I'm capable of at the moment.

- "Mistake" is a label I apply later.

- I can learn from my mistakes without guilt or worry.

- Everything I do is an effort to meet legitimate needs.

- I am letting go of unwise choices of the past.

- I can invent new ways to satisfy a need and wisely choose the best option.

Reframing Mistakes

• • • • • • • • • • • •

Just as the slimy, tentacled monster crawls over your face to implant its venom in your brain, you spring up in bed. Sweating, breathing hard, you realize that there is no monster—you've simply had a bad dream. You begin to relax, your breathing returns to normal, and you lie down. Everything's fine. It was only a nightmare.

When you reinterpret the experience of the monster crawling over your face as a nightmare, you're *reframing*—changing your interpretation or point of view. This is also a handy way to look at your mistakes. Instead of punishing yourself for mistakes, you can reframe them and put them to good use.

Think of mistakes as either lessons or warnings. Last year you decided not to go to the company picnic, and after you heard how much fun it had been, you regretted not going. Now, a year later, you look back on that mistake as a lesson and decide to go to this year's picnic.

A week ago you had your tires checked out, and the attendant told you the right front tire needed to be changed. The price seemed way too high to you, so you decided to put it off. Today, as you skid off the road after your tire blows, you realize that you probably should have replaced it. This mistake serves as a warning to attend to car maintenance a little more carefully.

Specific mistakes can give more general guidance about what to do the next time you're in a similar situation. The next time you're invited to a party and feel a little shy or lazy about going, you can think back to the missed picnic and make the decision to take a chance on having some fun. When your doctor tells you to get some exercise, maybe you can think back to your blown tire and decide to maintain yourself more carefully, too.

Go back to the list of your mistakes that you created for the exercise "Three Steps to Handling Mistakes." Look at each mistake listed and reframe it. What lesson did the mistake teach you? What do you know now about that error that you didn't know then? Did the mistake serve to warn you in future situations? Could it? Go through your list, marking "lesson" or "warning" next to each appropriate mistake. Take this opportunity to reframe your old mistakes, letting them work for rather than against you.

Escaping Your Past

· · · · · · · · · · ·

Do highly charged traumas from the past keep tripping you up in the present? If you have low self-esteem tied to especially painful memories, "gone" surely does not mean "forgotten." This imagery exercise dramatizes your escape from the past and reminds you that you actually have survived and made it to the safety of the present.

Lie down and close your eyes. Allow tight muscles to relax as you scan your body for tension. Let your breathing become slower and deeper. When you're relaxed, imagine that you are trudging across hot desert sands, dragging a huge cinder block chained to your ankle. The block and chain are past failures, fears, and disappointments that hold you back.

You come to an oasis where you meet a kindly old person with a hacksaw. The person, who reminds you of your favorite high school teacher, saws the chain off your ankle while you rest and drink cool water.

In the evening you continue on your journey. Shadows gather behind you and you realize that a crowd of ghosts is following you. They are people from the past who are now dead or otherwise absent from you life, but who continue to haunt you. You lead them into a deep cave, where you curl up and pretend to sleep. Just before dawn, you leave blankets curled in the shape of your old self and sneak out of the cave. You roll a rock over the mouth of the cave and it starts a landslide that buries and imprisons the ghosts forever.

You stride forward into the rising sun, turning on to a road. On the horizon you see your goal—the border line crossing into the kingdom of the present. If you can get that far, you'll be safe and free. But you notice other travelers coming up behind you, jostling you aside, slowing you as they pass. These are the people from your past who are still alive and present in your life. You have to deal with them.

You walk steadfastly onward, struggling to keep your balance in the crowd. Finally, you approach the border crossing. There are guards checking everybody's papers, turning everybody back. But you know the password: "This is now, that was then," and they let you through.

You reach the other side, safely arriving in the kingdom of the present. All the people from your past stare mournfully at you from the kingdom of the past. You can't even hear what they're saying anymore.

As you go about your routine the rest of they day, remind yourself that you live in the present now. You have escaped the past.

Visualizing Your Confident Self

· · · · · · · · ·

Christine hated visiting her in-laws. She felt awkward, trapped, and out of place in their living room, which hadn't changed since 1957. She felt like she just didn't fit in—she was too independent, too "modern." She always sensed a judgment coming from her mother-in-law, and that made her feel angry and ashamed.

Stan would do almost anything to avoid a first date. Though he'd been alone for about five years, and often found himself lonely and wishing he could find a partner, he simply couldn't stand the thought of that uncomfortable first date. The few times he'd been set up, the first encounter had made him squirm with insecurity.

Most people avoid certain situations that make them feel bad about themselves. Yet, many of these uncomfortable situations are necessary. Should Christine never go visit her in-laws? Her husband might have a big problem with that. Should Stan avoid dating altogether? Only if he's willing to be without a romantic partner for the rest of his life. Both of them need some tools to help them manage their discomfort in situations that make them feel unworthy.

If you have situations in your life that make you feel uncomfortable, the following visualization exercise will help you envision a confident you, a crucial first step to becoming the confident person you'd like to be.

Consider the various domains of your life: home, work, romance, friends, and so on. In each domain, pick a situation in which you feel uncomfortable, insecure, or ashamed.

Sit or lie down in a quiet place where you won't be disturbed. Close your eyes and breathe deeply. Consciously relax each muscle group in your body—your face, neck and shoulders, chest, stomach, pelvis, and legs.

Now, imagine the situation that makes you feel uncomfortable. Notice your surroundings—how do things look, sound, and smell? What do the people look like? What do you look like? What are you wearing? How do people respond to you? Take a deep breath and say to yourself, "I am calm and confident. I have a legitimate right to be here and be myself."

Keep imagining yourself in your chosen situation, and focus on your posture. See yourself standing or sitting tall, upright, and proud. Your back is straight, your shoulders are back, and you have a confident smile on your face. Think to yourself, "I am a valuable part of this encounter. I am confident that I belong here."

Notice how, when you add to the conversation, the people with you respond positively, nodding their heads and smiling at you. They are happy that you're there and respect your opinion. Now imagine saying or doing something a little risky, something that might bring a negative reaction. See the other people in the room stop to consider what you've said or done, then nod their heads in approval as slow smiles spread across their faces. Take a deep breath, saying to yourself, "I am successful in this situation." See yourself sitting up even straighter and smiling broadly. You are now at home here.

Repeat this visualization for each domain you've chosen. If you practice for at least four days, you will likely find that you will begin to behave the way you do in the visualization—and people will respond to you in kind. Remember, in some senses, you *are* who you *believe* you are.

Turn Offs and Turn Ons

· · · · · · · · · · · · ·

Have you ever had a dream in which you were struggling to read something or understand a long conversation? You can't seem to make out the words. That's because your unconscious mind doesn't understand words very well, preferring to deal with symbols and images. This visualization uses symbols to tell your unconscious mind to turn off negative self-concepts and turn on self-esteem.

Lie down and close your eyes. Scan your body for tension, willing tight muscles to loosen and relax. Breathe more slowly and deeply. Tell yourself, "I am getting more and more relaxed with each passing moment."

When you feel calm and at peace, imagine that your body is like a tall building with many levels and rooms. In the basement there's a control room that regulates all the electricity, water, gas, air-conditioning, phone lines, and so on. Locate that control room in your building and open the door with a key you find in your pocket.

Walk into the control room and turn left. There are many dusty, rusted plumbing pipes coming up from the floor and exiting out the ceiling, studded with several faucets and valves. These are the pipes that supply your negative self-image, your self-doubt, and your timidity. Walk up to the pipes and shut off each valve or faucet tightly, turning the wheels and handles firmly clockwise and shutting off the flow. Then cross over to the right side of the room, where a neat and tidy array of new pipes is waiting. Turn on all the new faucets and valves, starting the flow of positive self-image, confidence, and assurance.

Return to the left side of the room and open a battered metal door on the electrical box. Inside you see many black plastic-and-chrome metal switches, all in the ON position. One by one, flip them to OFF, cutting the power to your shyness circuit, your procrastination circuit, your perfectionism circuit, and so on. There's a thick cable coming out of the top of the box, the main negative power feed. Take a fire ax from the wall and sever the cable in a satisfying shower of sparks. Now cross over to the right side of the room and open your new power box. Use both hands to throw the huge main switch to ON. Click each separate new switch to ON to power up your affection, self-love, tolerance, pride, and so on.

Back on the left wall, there's an old-fashioned telephone switchboard with lots of cords patched into various ongoing conversations with your pathological critic. Pull out all the cords and leave them hanging in midair. Cross over to the right side and plug a new, modern phone into the simple wall jack that connects you to a reasonable assessment of your worth.

On the left wall is a blaring public address system calling you names. Turn it off. On the right wall is a nice stereo system. Turn it on and soft music starts to play—someone singing you a love song. There are several slider switches like the ones that control left and right stereo speakers. The slider switches control your view of the past, your concern for the future, your reliance on the opinions of others, and so on. Slide all the switches to the center, BALANCED position.

When all the switches, valves, and controls in this room are set to your satisfaction, lock the door and leave. You can always return later if something gets out of adjustment.

Remind yourself of your surroundings and open your eyes. Congratulate yourself on a message well sent to your unconscious mind.

PART VIII

Minimize Judgments

Making judgments is necessary to your survival. Humans sort everything they see, hear, taste, and smell into three categories: irrelevant, good, and bad. You ignore the irrelevant, seek the good, and avoid the bad. You can't stop making judgments. If you did, you'd starve, get run over, or walk off a cliff.

The problem comes when you form a habit of sorting yourself into the "bad" pile. You can't avoid yourself for long. You eventually have to face your negative self-judgments. That's the essence of poor self-esteem—coming face-to-face with your "bad" self.

Think of your own experience. Suppose you miss a deadline or do a job that has errors. The impulse to kick yourself around is probably huge and stems from the hope that the attack will somehow make you different, make you a person who no longer feels this worthlessness.

Using judgment as a tool to perfect ourselves is addictive—and poisonous. The truth is that compulsive self-judgment doesn't help anyone to be better. All it does is kill your self-esteem.

This section explains how you make judgments, why negative self-judgments persist, and how to make more accurate and positive judgments of yourself and others.

The Screens in Your Head

· · · · · · · · · · · · · · · · ·

We all select, alter, and distort what we see. You filter and edit reality as if your eyes and ears were a TV camera and you were seeing reality on a screen in your head. Sometimes your camera zooms in on certain details, like seeing your boss's brow furrow as he or she reads your report. Your camera may magnify or minimize according to your inner critic's beliefs about your abilities. Or perhaps your camera puts in an old tape, and lo and behold, you perceive reality based entirely on old experiences, without even realizing it.

For instance, Seth finally decided to ask the girl at the coffee shop out on a date. He'd been trying to build up the nerve for weeks. His friends insisted that she always smiled at him with a brighter, I'd-love-to-go-out-with-that-guy kind of smile, but all Seth could feel were his old doubts and fears rising in his chest as he neared the shop. Suddenly he was there, face-to-face with her. She was smiling. He was wearing his coolest loafers. It was time.

"Hi, would you like to go to the beach with me? I mean the bench?"

What the hell was that?! Seth actually meant the bench outside, just to sit and chat, but it came out sounding absurd. All he could think was, "She must think I'm a total fool." She quickly looked at the customer behind him and said, "Hi, uh, can I help you?"

Seth was in shock. She just totally ignored him. She also looked a little scared, so he assumed she thought he was a psychopath. She dropped the next customer's latte into the bagel platter, and Seth was convinced that it was because she was so freaked out by his bungled move. Swallowing the lump in his throat, he walked over to the napkin dispenser and stared at his pathetic reflection in the shiny little metal dispenser. Then he saw someone else's warped eye reflecting there too. It was her!

"Hi. I'm sorry—my manager came in just as you asked me to go to the, uh, beach or bench, and I get really nervous when he's around. So, anyway, I'd love to hang out with you sometime!" It wasn't Seth at all! She was really scared of her boss! Seth was simply reading all of his fears into her actions. He had no way of realizing that what he was filtering onto his screen was not reality.

Here's an exercise to help you become aware of how you filter reality through the TV screen in your head:

1. Remember a recent, painful interaction with another person. Write down what you both said and did.

2. Write down what you assume the other person was seeing and hearing about you on their screen. What might they have been projecting that led to their words and actions?

3. Re-run the scene in your mind, looking for missed data. Find actions and words that might give you a new slant on the situation. Look especially for things you ignored or disbelieved the first time.

4. Write down an alternative explanation of what the other person may have seen and heard on their screen.

Rules about Screens

. . . .

Your screen is not always a bad thing. It merely reflects the way your senses and your mind are wired together. You need this filter—how else could you organize the flood of information coming at you all the time? However, because you always interpret reality through the TV screen in your head, you can't rely on what you're viewing to be the "truth." And you have no way of knowing what's really on someone else's screen! To make matters even trickier, it's impossible to fully communicate what's on your screen, since some of what's there is unconscious material.

Take Mary, who's out to dinner with her sweetheart, Stan. She tells him about her day at work and how everyone is an imbecile but her. She's totally absorbed in the events she's recounting, slapping her hands on the table, throwing things around, practically putting on a napkin puppet show to demonstrate the full drama of her work environment.

She takes a moment to glance over at her partner, just to make sure Stan is grasping the entirety of this outrage, and he looks like he just swallowed a tranquilizer. He's resting his head in hands as if he's about to drop off. It's even possible that he's secretly perusing the dessert card on the table. The nerve! He's almost as bad as Mary's father, who never responded with much more than a grunt or guffaw at the family dinner table. "Who are these uncaring, uncompassionate, bored men I seem to surround myself with?" she asks herself.

Then he actually speaks. "Uh, honey, I got fired today. Sorry if I'm not too engaged. I'm feeling really down. The truth is, it's kind of comforting just listening to you tell your stories—it's helping me not get too absorbed in my depression. Thanks." All Mary can think is, "Oh, jeez. I had that all wrong."

When you realize that you can't automatically believe what's on your screen, you can do something about it. You're better equipped for the next situation—now you know you can always stop and reevaluate your initial reaction. Following is an exercise to help you become aware of how you filter reality through the TV screen in your head.

For the rest of today or all day tomorrow, imagine that your eyes are a camera. Your ears are microphones. Be the director of a documentary. Consciously compose a voice-over commentary on what you see and hear. Shift your attention to emphasize the negative or positive aspects of a scene. When someone says something to you, pretend that both of you are characters in a movie. Imagine several responses besides the one you would normally give. Imagine several possible motivations for what other people do besides the motives you assume are correct.

Notice how this distancing exercise changes your awareness of reality. It can help you realize that there are many more possible ways to see reality than the one you usually use. It should also point out how automatic and limited your usual perception of the world can be.

Screens as Monster Makers

· · · · · · · · · · · · · · · · · ·

Your screen is your interpretation of reality—you manipulate what you see, filtering out either the positive or the negative. Your perceptions are based on what you expect to see and what you have seen before.

Sometimes your insecurities can dominate your filtering system, making a monster out of just about anyone. And certain situations will bring out your skewed interpretations more than others. When you're feeling awkward or unsure of yourself, everyday encounters can seem like veiled attacks. You can make a monster out of a friendly and blameless stranger.

For example, Leah attended her new boyfriend's art opening in a swanky downtown art gallery. She was already feeling a little tense in anticipation of incomprehensible art discussions. Although she usually felt confident and secure with her career in social work, Bob's art crowd always triggered her monster alert—suddenly everyone became a potential attacker out to make her feel stupid. Leah didn't like feeling this way, but when her insecurities took charge, she was at their mercy.

Almost immediately, a six-foot-tall woman wearing all black approached Leah, blew the smoke from her Euro-import cigarette in Leah's face, and asked, "So, what brings you here?"

With this tower of sophistication leering down on her, poor Leah felt like a country bumpkin, masquerading in her fancy duds for the evening. Without thinking, she blurted, "I'm here for the pretty pictures, what's it to ya?" Leah felt her whole face flush as she saw the woman's surprised face. The monster that she'd created out of this woman instantly evaporated. Suddenly she was just a person trying to make conversation. The woman backed up slowly and excused herself saying, "Oh, I see, well, it was nice meeting you."

Most people have experienced a gaffe similar to this. No one feels secure and confident in every situation. But when you're feeling this way, you should try to reconsider the reality you're perceiving on your screen. You can usually tell when your insecurities are dictating your emotions because you'll feel fear. Maybe you'll have a tense stomach, short rapid breathing, or weak knees.

While you're at home, safe from any real attackers, imagine a scenario that you know would make you feel unsure of yourself. Imagine your body tensing as you look around at all the possible monsters. Then ask yourself, "Are my feelings right now linked to reality?" Picture someone in the scene asking you a simple question such as "What brings you here?" or "What do you do for a living?" Do you feel anxious just imagining this? If so, you can be pretty sure that you're expecting everybody to be a monster.

Responding to
Others' Judgments

· · · · · · · · · · ·

When others are judging you, you need to ask, "What are they perceiving about me? Is it linked to reality? What's on their screen?" Remember that everyone interprets reality through the TV screen in their heads. A critic is only being critical of the content of his or her own screen, not of reality. It has nothing to do with you directly. However, it's easy to forget this and to allow your inner critic to automatically agree. Don't give in at the first sign of an attack.

There are essentially two types of criticism: destructive and constructive. To respond assertively, you need to determine a few things. Does the critic want to help or hassle you? This requires probing until the intention becomes clear. For example, if your partner tells you you've "let her down," you need to ask for specifics so that you're both viewing the same channel on your screens. You can ask, "How exactly have I let you down? Can you give me some examples?" As you gather the facts, you'll be able to determine the critic's intent. If there are accurate, valid points, you can simply acknowledge them, apologize, and then develop a plan for changing. That is enough.

However, if the critic is out to vent some of his or her own unrelated frustrations, you need to know this, too. This is destructive criticism. This critic deserves the clouding response. In this case, you can agree in part or in principle, but stop there. It's like saying to your critic, "Okay, some of what is on your screen is also on my screen. And some isn't." This is effective assertiveness—you counter someone's inaccurate criticism without being defensive and exacerbating the tension.

For instance, your parent says, "I can't believe you took the writing job at the nonprofit agency—you'll never make enough money there to support yourself and a family! What are you going to do in ten years when you have nothing saved up and a lousy little nonprofit, leftist company on your résumé?" You respond by saying, "Yeah, it's true that this agency is never going to pay me enough to support what you consider to be a comfortable, successful lifestyle. But I believe in their cause."

This type of clouding response says to your critic, "Maybe you're right, but I intend to exercise my right to my own opinion." You've acknowledged the unwelcome criticism, and your self-esteem is still intact.

Recall a recent encounter you've had with criticism. Was the critic out to help or hassle you? Was the criticism intended to be constructive and accurate or destructive and distorted? To answer these questions, you may have to do some after-the-fact probing. Try to recall any facts or specifics offered by the critic that indicate whether their intent was constructive or destructive.

If the criticism seemed accurate, did you acknowledge it? If it wasn't accurate, did you counter it? Reconstruct the scene in your mind. Visualize yourself handling it in a way that now seems more productive. Imagine probing to figure out your critic's intention and then responding accordingly. If there was some validity, remember that all you need to do is acknowledge, apologize, and then stop.

If the criticism was inaccurate or destructive, imagine using the clouding method in dealing with the confrontation. Who needs unnecessary criticism? Not you!

Reflecting Others' Admirable Qualities

• • • • • • • • • • •

Sherry surveyed the party going on around her as she sank deep into the couch with her drink. Wow—everyone there was so "on," so alive and sociable. There was Mark cracking jokes like always, busting everyone up. And Marsha, deeply involved in another intellectual conversation with her classmate, Roy. Paul, gracefully taking care of everyone's needs without ever seeming intrusive. Sarah, sending folks into hysterics with another one of her impressions.

Sherry was really proud of her friends—they all had such wonderful talents and personalities. As she took a long drink from her gin and tonic she sank deeper into the couch and wondered why all these exceptional people were friends with *her*? She was pretty commonplace in comparison.

Have you ever felt like Sherry, looking around at friends you admire and wondering why they would deign to talk to you? Or are you shy with folks you don't know well but admire? Are you reluctant to approach them, thinking that maybe you can't "match up"? Have you ever considered that they might feel the same way about you? If so, try the following exercise.

Make a list of five people you admire. They can be people you know personally or public figures. Next, for each of the five people you've chosen, list the qualities in them that you most appreciate. Perhaps they have a good sense of humor, a strong sense of responsibility, a creative flair, a logical mind, or a fair nature. Maybe they have succeeded in their career or are loving parents. The traits you list can be anything you find admirable.

Now, look carefully at the qualities you've come up with for each person. Which of these apply to you? Think carefully before you decide. Remember how very easy it is to see good qualities in others and remain utterly oblivious to them in yourself. If it helps, pretend you are your own best friend. What would your best friend say your good qualities are? Are you a faithful friend? Are you funny? Do you come through in a pinch? Think carefully and as fairly as you can.

Finally, review the good qualities you've acknowledged in yourself and think of the last episode in which each quality was evident. As you remember, take time to give yourself credit. Remember others' reactions to this quality in you. Remember how it felt to possess this quality. Enjoy the memory.

Learning to Be Nonjudgmental

· · · · · · · · · ·

Pathological judgments are poison. They are like pouring acid over a bouquet of roses or drinking lemonade spiked with arsenic. Pathological judgments are based on the belief that things are intrinsically good or bad, right or wrong, black or white. They're poison because every absolute judgment you apply to your friends, your lover, or someone you read about in the paper can come back to haunt you. The paradox is that your harsh standards seldom influence others, but often diminish you, because it is impossible to live up to your standards all the time.

For example, Susan worked with a woman named Uma, of whom she strongly disapproved. Uma was beautiful, funny, flirtatious, and married. Susan was attractive, smart, and married, but felt superior in her ability to exhibit absolutely no sexual attraction for anyone other than her stunning husband, Bob. Susan watched every morning as Uma came into the office wearing a skirt above her knee or a shirt that was a little too snug. Susan's lips would tighten and she would think, "Uma is such a hussy. I feel sorry for her poor husband—I wonder if he knows what kind of woman he's married to!"

Uma, on the other hand, would smile at Susan each morning, asking her about Bob or how her job was going. Even though Uma always received the same tepid response from Susan, she showed no signs of letting it get to her. Meanwhile, Susan would go home at night and tell Bob about what Uma wore at work that day or how long she talked to a male co-worker at the water fountain, forgetting to mention that Uma talked to almost everyone at the water fountain.

Then one day Susan's firm hired a man named Tony who took a liking to her. Tony was also married, but he still found Susan funny and interesting. They shared interests in professional bowling and rare coins. He had a harmless and platonic admiration for Susan, but she felt uncomfortable when he asked her what she was doing for lunch. When Susan found herself wondering what Tony was doing for lunch, she immediately felt *wrong*.

The unreasonably high standards she set for others caused her to feel that now she was a "hussy" herself, just because she liked a male in the office. Susan felt guilty, as if she were somehow injuring Bob by being friendly with Tony. She grew cooler toward Tony, and he eventually stopped asking her whether she had caught the previous evening's tournament or what she was doing for lunch.

Susan failed to realize that most personal choices are based on needs and tastes, not on morality. You can avoid this worldview by developing the awareness that everyone chooses *the highest perceived good*. Here are a couple of things you can do to develop a nonjudgmental attitude:

- Practice reading the newspaper without making a single judgment about any of the behavior reported in any story. Take the position (even if you don't fully believe it) that each person is choosing the highest good based on his or her current awareness.

- When you see people wearing unattractive clothes or hairstyles, or whose physical appearance is not to your taste, practice this mantra: "He or she is blameless for any choices that created his or her appearance."

Learning Empathy

. . . .

Walter and his friend, Jeff, emerge onto the sunny street after watching one of the new summer movie releases, *Vast Chasm*. Jeff loved it—the meteor, the monsters, the beautiful heroine. Unfortunately, Walter can't say he feels the same way, and now it seems as if a vast chasm is opening up between them.

As Jeff strides along, celebrating the fantastic special effects, Walter finds himself judging Jeff's taste in movies—and Jeff himself. And, in his condemnation of Jeff, Walter also comes down hard on himself. After all, he is Jeff's friend. What does that say about his taste in people?

Walter is suffering from a lack of empathy, which is the attempt to truly understand another's feelings. What if, instead of closing his mind to Jeff's feelings, Walter set aside his judgments and tried to understand where Jeff was coming from? With a little empathy, Walter might conclude that Jeff has some good reasons for his preference. Walter would then be free to respect the differences between himself and his friend without condemning either of them. And, as a bonus, he might even be able to actually enjoy going to the movies with Jeff again.

The following exercise provides an easy, nonthreatening way to practice the vital skill of empathy (crucial in the development of compassion for yourself and others). All you need for the exercise is a chair, a TV, and an open mind.

Turn on the TV and immediately switch the channel to a show you absolutely hate—something you normally wouldn't be caught dead watching (don't worry—you can draw the blinds so the neighbors won't know).

Watch and listen carefully. Every time you feel irritated, disgusted, bored, or embarrassed, try to set your feelings aside and refocus your attention on the show. Say to yourself, "I notice I'm feeling very irritated by this. That's okay, but it's not what I'm interested in right now. I can set this irritation aside and just observe for a while without judging."

Suspend your value judgments for a time and imagine why the faithful fans watch this show. What do they get out of it? Do they watch for excitement, enlightenment, or escape? Try to understand the attractive features of the show and what kind of person likes it.

When you have a good idea about what makes the show fascinating for some people (when you've reached an empathetic understanding), switch channels and try it again. Remember, you don't have to approve or disapprove of what you're watching—just try to see it clearly and understand its attractions.

The goal of this exercise isn't to expand or corrupt your viewing taste. The purpose is to provide a safe, nonthreatening opportunity for you to practice setting aside your snap judgments and to gain an understanding of a viewpoint you ordinarily might dismiss immediately. Give it a try—and then maybe you'll want to call your friend for a trip to the movies.

Kicking the Judgment Habit

· · · · · · · · · · · · · · · · · ·

Some families are so critical that their children grow up feeling bad and unworthy. Daily emotional slaps and dings add up to a feeling that there is something wrong with you. If you come from such a family, you know the feelings don't end when you finally escape to live on your own.

You still feel wrong and bad. And there's a voice inside that keeps attacking you—just like your parents did. It's as if you've taken their judgments with you, a dark inheritance from early family life. This habit of self-attack comes from the same belief your parents had—that emotional beatings will correct your flaws, punish your sins, and shape you into a finer human being. But it didn't work then, and it isn't working now. All it does is chip away at your self-esteem.

Paradoxically, self-attacks and judgments are born from hope—the hope that everything you hate in yourself can be beaten into a more ideal shape. And with your new perfected self, the old feelings of being bad and wrong will finally heal. This hope can be addictive. Each self-attack holds the promise of somehow making you acceptable in your own eyes. It's hard to stop—because if you cease the self-attacks, it feels as if you'll lose your only chance to ever feel worthy.

When you honestly examine your experience, you know this isn't true. The judgments only tear you down. Never once have they brought you closer to feeling good about yourself. You need to kick the judgment habit. Try the following exercises to help you achieve abstinence from self-attack.

Ironically, the first step in overcoming self-attack is to change your pattern of judging *others*. For the next week, listen to the radio news without making a single judgment about any of the behavior reported in any story. Tell yourself that everyone is doing the best they can, given their fears, needs, skills, pain, and personal history.

Continue to work on the temptation to judge others by calling up a family member whose opinions often raise your hackles. Throughout the conversation practice a nonjudging attitude. Refrain from judging anything this person says as right or wrong, good or bad.

Recall a scene from the past when you felt very wrong and bad about yourself. Relive the scene moment by moment. See the action; hear the dialogue. But this time experience the events without judgment. Be aware of how your needs, fears, skills, pain, and history shaped your choices. Notice yourself, at the time, doing your best. Repeat this exercise with at least three additional scenes.

The Tyranny of the Shoulds

. . . .

Alice was a bad mother. At least that's what she kept thinking as she moved through her Friday afternoon at work. As she attended her weekly staff meeting and made the presentation she'd been preparing for all week, all she could think about was how she'd failed her son, Sammy, by not going to his school play that afternoon. She thought to herself: "What kind of a mother misses her son's starring role in his third grade play? A bad mother, that's what kind."

Alice is suffering under the crushing weight of her own *shoulds*. She believes that a good mother *should* attend all of her children's school functions, no matter what. She feels it's a cop-out to ever put her job before Sammy, so when she has to miss the play in favor of presenting to her company, she is wracked with guilt. It doesn't matter that she threw Sammy a birthday party the previous weekend, or that she'd gone to almost all of his other school events, or even that Sammy's dad would be there. She was convinced that her missing this school play meant that she was a bad mom.

Maybe you also operate under a list of shoulds that dictate how you *should* behave. Inevitably, you're unable to live up to all of your shoulds. When that happens, you might take the opportunity to beat yourself up, deciding that you're wrong, bad, or weak, torturing yourself with guilt and self-blame.

Most people hold a list of shoulds in their heart and use these shoulds as a series of impossible hurdles that they have to surmount each day. Many folks don't even know exactly what their shoulds are or whether these shoulds make sense in their lives. Below you'll find a list of the most common pathological shoulds. Consider each one carefully, and put a check by the shoulds that may apply to you. Later on you'll learn to evaluate them to see if they make sense for your life.

_____ I should be the epitome of generosity and unselfishness.

_____ I should be the perfect lover, partner, worker, friend, parent, teacher, student, etc.

_____ I should be able to endure any hardship with composure and a sense of balance.

_____ I should be able to find a quick solution to every problem.

_____ I should never feel hurt. I should always feel happy and serene.

_____ I should be completely competent.

_____ I should know, foresee, and understand everything.

_____ I should never feel certain emotions, such as anger or jealousy.

_____ I should love my children equally.

_____ I should never make mistakes.

_____ My emotions should remain constant—once I feel love, I should always feel love.

_____ I should be totally self-reliant.

_____ I should never be tired or sick.

_____ I should never be afraid.

_____ I should have achievements that bring me status, wealth, or power.

_____ I should always be busy; relaxing wastes my time and my life.

_____ I should put others first; it is better to feel pain than to cause others pain.

_____ I should be unfailingly kind.

_____ I should never feel sexually attracted to _____ .

_____ I should care for everyone who cares for me.

_____ I should make enough money so my family can afford _____ .

_____ I should be able to protect my children from all pain.

_____ I should not take time just for my own pleasure.

Once you've reviewed the list and checked the appropriate items, you're ready to move on to the next exercise—replacing your shoulds with healthier values.

Healthy Versus
Unhealthy Values

. . . .

Your beliefs, values, and shoulds help define who you are and who you understand yourself to be. But where did these beliefs, values, and shoulds come from?

Most beliefs are formed in response to some basic human need—the need for acceptance, love, comfort, or sustenance. Your first beliefs came from your need to be approved of by your parents. In order to feel safe and cared for, you adopted your parents' beliefs about such things as work; how to handle anger, mistakes, and pain; what one can and cannot talk about; what are the proper goals of life; what is owed to parents and other family members; and how self-reliant a person should be. A lot of these beliefs were probably promoted using value-laden words like commitment, intelligence, and/or strength. Your parents applied these words (or their negative opposites) to you and others who did or didn't live up to specific rules. In your need to please your parents, you tended to accept their evaluation of others—especially their assessment and consequent judgments of you.

A second group of beliefs come from the need to feel belonging or approval from peers. To make sure you get the acceptance you need, you learn to live by the rules and beliefs of your group—rules about how to act with romantic partners, how to handle aggression or anger, how much of yourself to reveal to others, and what are appropriate sex-role behaviors.

The third major force that helps to shape your beliefs is the need for emotional and physical well-being. This is a group of needs including the need for self-esteem; the need to protect yourself from hurt or loss; the need for pleasure, excitement, or meaning; and the need to feel physically safe.

These are some of the needs that helped you form the beliefs, values, and shoulds by which you live. But sometimes you may find yourself operating under beliefs that no longer fit the life you lead now. You may be knocking your head against limiting beliefs that were formed in response to needs that no longer exist (like the need to be protected by your parents). These rules and beliefs are no longer appropriate and can damage your self-worth.

The good news is that you are *always* free to reevaluate your beliefs, rules, and values—and to change them if necessary. The following criteria can help you decide whether your values are appropriate for the life you're living now.

Healthy values are flexible. Unhealthy values are rigid, often including words like *never*, *always*, *all*, and *perfectly*. Flexible rules allow for exceptions, while unhealthy rules are unbending and universally applied. Flexible rules include a built-in awareness that a certain percentage of the time you will fail to live up to the ideal standard.

Healthy values are owned rather than introjected. *Owning* a belief means that you've critically examined it, and it still makes sense to you. The *introjected belief* is one you accepted from your parents without determining how well it fits your personality, circumstances, and needs.

Healthy values are positive. A positive value or rule promotes behavior that leads to positive outcomes. It will encourage you to do things that will result in long-term happiness for all people involved. Healthy values are life enhancing rather than life restricting. This means that the rules you live by must take into account your basic needs as a human being. Life-enhancing values encourage you to do what is nourishing and supportive, except in situations where long-term consequences are painful for yourself and others.

After reading the criteria for healthy versus unhealthy values, go to the shoulds checklist from the previous exercise ("The Tyranny of the Shoulds") and evaluate the shoulds you checked for yourself. Are your shoulds flexible, owned, realistic, and life enhancing?

Causes and Effects
of Self-Esteem

• • • • • • • • •

According to developmental psychologists, if you had critical, neglectful, or abusive parents, you probably started life with low self-esteem. But after age four or five, another factor comes into play that determines your adult self-worth.

For years social scientists have debated causes and effects. Does academic success raise self-esteem or does high self-esteem lead to academic success? Does high social status cause high self-worth, or does high self-worth help you gain high social status?

These are classic cause-and-effect, chicken-and-egg questions that miss the main point: It's not the *facts* of your life that determine how you feel about yourself. It's which facts you choose to think about and believe. For example, if you look in the mirror and think, "Boy am I fat! What a slob!" you will clobber your self-esteem. On the other hand, you give your self-esteem a boost if you look in the mirror and think, "My hair looks good!" Same mirror, same person, same facts—different thoughts.

The key to raising your self-esteem is really that simple: you change how you feel about yourself by changing how you think about yourself. Simple doesn't mean easy or quick. You won't change the mental habits of a lifetime in the time it takes to read this page. But you can start right now.

Think of a famous person you admire. Write down three facts about that person's life that you associate with high self-esteem. For example, if you chose a movie star, you might write that she is beautiful, funny, and free spirited. Now write another three facts about this person that you associate with low self-esteem. This may be harder. What do you know about this person's life that indicates that it's not all a bed of roses? The movie stars may be beautiful, but they seem to go under the knife for plastic surgery regularly to stay that way. They may be funny but also have a drug problem. Their free spirit may have led them through multiple failed marriages because they can never seem to settle down.

Repeat the same exercise, listing three positive and three negative facts about a friend. This will probably be easier, since you know more about a friend's life. Then try it with yourself. List three facts about your life that make you feel better about yourself and then three facts that seem to lower your self-esteem.

This exercise shows how easily you can tilt your reaction and feeling about anyone—simply by choosing to focus on a different set of facts.

Goals Visualization

• • • • • • • • • • •

Setting and achieving goals can give a big boost to your self-esteem. Visualization is one of the most successful tools for clarifying your goals and creating an expectation for accomplishment. You can redefine your self-image and make important changes in your life through the simple steps of relaxing your body, clearing your mind of distractions, and imagining positive scenes.

Start simple—pick the kind of everyday goals that you tend to beat yourself up about: exercising a certain amount each week, organizing your financial records, writing important letters, and so on. This is much more effective than visualizing yourself having achieved grandiose accomplishments or made lots of money twenty years from now.

For example, suppose your goal is to get up well-rested and make it to work on time each morning. Sit or lie down in a quiet place and do your favorite relaxation exercise. When you're in a suggestible frame of mind, imagine the following scene:

First, imagine yourself getting to bed at a reasonable time the night before, perhaps reading in bed and drifting calmly off to sleep. The alarm clock goes off. You are well rested and simply turn off the clock, avoiding the usual temptation to hit the snooze button. You get right out of bed, stretch your arms up over your head, and let out one deep breath.

Continue with your usual routine. Imagine yourself taking a shower, allowing yourself time to feel how invigorating the hot water is. You climb out of the shower, dry off, and then put on your most comfortable work clothes. Soft cotton, thick socks, and maybe your favorite sweater. After dressing, you eat a healthy breakfast. Finally, you pick up your bag or briefcase, which you've already packed up the night before, and leave with plenty of time to get where you're going on schedule. Imagine your car starting right up or catching the earlier bus rather than the last-chance bus that ordinarily gets you across town five minutes too late.

Throughout this scene, add details that show you are relaxed, unhurried, and efficient. For example, you find your keys just where you placed them when you came home the night before. Say to yourself, "I'm organized and punctual."

You might even invent a few obstacles, such as hearing the phone ring or having the newspaper deliverer drop by to collect the monthly payment. See yourself calmly cutting the phone call short or quickly writing the paper deliverer a check. Tell yourself, "I can stay calm and focused and still make it to work on time."

Visualize the positive benefits of arriving at work on time. There is still time for you to make a cup of coffee or tea, sit down, and organize yourself for the day. Co-workers are pleased and feel they can approach you with questions without worrying about stressing you out. You're off to a good start!

Before leaving this scene, tell yourself that you will initiate this sequence, starting tonight when you get home. Now, when you're ready, take a deep breath and open your eyes.

Try imagining other scenes using this same progression. Maybe you have a deadline approaching, some filing to do, or a job for which you'd like to apply. Remember to keep your goals simple and short-term at first. The self-esteem boosts you get from achieving small goals will give you the confidence you need to set and accomplish bigger, more long-term goals.

Matthew McKay, Ph.D., is a professor at the Wright Institute in Berkeley, CA. He is the author and coauthor of more than twenty-five books, including *The Relaxation and Stress Reduction Workbook, Thoughts and Feelings, Messages, When Anger Hurts, Self-Esteem* and *The Self-Esteem Guided Journal*. He received his Ph.D. in clinical psychology from the California School of Professional Psychology. In private practice, he specializes in the cognitive behavioral treatment of anxiety, anger, and depression.

Patrick Fanning is a professional writer in the mental health field and the founder of a men's support group in Northern California. He is the coauthor of eight self-help books, including: *Messages, Self-Esteem, Thoughts and Feelings,* and *Couple Skills*

Carole Honeychurch, M.A., is a freelance writer, www.iVillage.com relationship expert, and coauthor of *Talk to Me, After the Breakup,* and *Love Tune-Ups*. She lives in the San Francisco Bay Area.

Catharine Sutker is a freelance writer living in the San Francisco Bay Area. She is the coauthor of *The Self-Nourishment Companion, The Self-Esteem Companion,* and *The Self-Esteem Guided Journal*.

Also Available

SELF-ESTEEM, THIRD EDITION

MATTHEW MCKAY, PH.D. • PATRICK FANNING

With over 600,000 copies sold, this classic has long been the most comprehensive guide on the subject. Proven cognitive techniques help you talk back to the self-critical voice inside you and change the ways you think and feel about yourself.

ISBN 1-57224-198-5 / US $15.95

THE SELF-ESTEEM GUIDED JOURNAL

A 10-Week Program

MATTHEW MCKAY, PH.D. • CATHARINE SUTKER

From the authors of *Self-Esteem*, *The Self-Esteem Guided Journal* offers readers a ten-week writing program to shift their focus from the things wrong with their lives to the things that are right. This book uses a technique known as guided journaling to help readers teach themselves to vocalize their feelings, conquer self-doubt, discover their strengths—and generally change the way they think and feel about themselves for the better.

ISBN 1-57224-402-X / US $13.95